A World Without Fear

Cover design: Doug Gobel / GobelDesign.com

Bio Photograph By: Geoffrey Baris / GeoffreyBarisArt.Com

Contents

Introduction:

I am a Life Coach, spiritual counselor and spiritual teacher. I work with hundreds of clients and their relatives on all of the most difficult of life's issues. In the process I have learned a great deal from my clients about fear and pain and how it affects people's lives. The fear release and negative emotion release techniques and concepts included in this work-book were developed as a result of my interactions with these clients, and have been applied repeatedly and successfully.

Many of my clients have lived with the detrimental effects of fear, conflict, trauma and abuse in every area of their lives. Whether the fears they were dealing with were their own or fears held by someone they were in relationship with, or both. Their willingness to courageously work through the most difficult aspects of their life experiences has helped me to construct the deeper understandings of how all negative emotions such as anger, jealousy, hatred, aggression, guilt and shame are simply the result and reflections of unresolved deeply rooted fears. We only feel these other negative emotional states if we *first* feel a deep sense of fear of something. These secondary negative emotions are in effect a sort of defensive reaction to our underlying fear; they are our way of trying to "manage our fear", cope with it, or in some cases hide from it. If we find *some other* way of resolving the fear then the secondary negative emotions go away immediately. This is why fear release techniques, and working with our fears directly, is so important and why it brings such relief in so many areas of our lives.

I have four main goals in writing this book:

- To offer the reader methods of understanding, working with and releasing fear and other negative emotional states. (It is my personal intention to help you free yourself from all of the fears that limit you from achieving your life goals in a healthy and wisdom producing manner).
- To offer the reader the opportunity to find new joy in their lives via learning to view all of life from the vantage point of gratitude. (This can occur after you *cease* viewing life from the vantage point of fear or any other negative emotional vantage point).
- To empower the reader to leave behind whatever limitations their past experiences may have placed upon them, and guide them to fearlessly and joyfully manifest whatever they desire in their lives.
- To reduce human emotional suffering and conflict individually and globally.

The various chapters of this book focus on ways to approach each of these goals, and over time and with practice to achieve them. In order to live life joyfully and to our fullest, as well as to achieve some semblance of inner maintainable peace, it is necessary to have a personal *system of emotional self-management*. Most people are not taught how to either understand or to manage their emotions by their families or society's educational system. We are not taught to understand our emotional selves or manage our emotional selves in any standardized or effective way. We *are often taught* to suppress and painfully endure our negative emotions, or to judge them, deny them, to be angry about them or even to hate our own emotions. We are also taught to act out on them in detrimental ways that damage our relationships or our lives. Over time we may become numb to our own emotional process, this is especially true of males who may have been taught that to be emotionally sensitive or expressive is a sign of weakness. We are also taught to react in many maladaptive ways in regard to *other's* negative emotions, rather than responding with constructive tolerance and conscious helpful action.

This way of interacting with our own negative emotions in general is not in our best interest and has led to vast suffering in the history of humanity. Various techniques have been developed to help people with their negative emotions, including "mindfulness meditation", which has been around for thousands of years. Yet these self-management methods are still not broadly taught to the general population of the world and so everyone continues to stress and emotionally suffer to some degree without direct effective relief. In addition, these methods may not appear to fit well with today's fast paced high pressure lifestyles, or may be looked upon as "new age" or eccentric. In today's world that which is either not based in science or modern medicine is often dismissed, unfortunately science is not focusing enough on resolving the fear and emotional suffering of humanity. Paradoxically medical science is finding direct connections between stress, negative emotions and their detrimental effects on physical health and healing. In fact the methods listed in this book are very applicable and practical, if we simply choose to make the decision to implement them in our lives, in an intentional and willful manner.

Many of us struggle with the discipline necessary to accomplish consistent positive changes in our lives and this is part of the problem. As I describe later in the book a key part of managing the implementation of these kinds of positive changes is dealing with the fear and stress that making *any kind of change* in our stress filled lives produces. That is why it is so important to have effective methods that are simple and work. It is also why it is important to be able to release fears *rapidly and in the moment* when you are trying to implement positive change in your life is so important and why it is important to have simple effective techniques for doing so.

We can learn to become consciously aware of the detrimental emotional domino effects created by our fears and the disruptive dynamics they create in our lives and relationships. When we do understand the *process of fear* and how it creates all of our other negative emotions we can then realize the benefit and necessity of becoming aware of and clearing our fears. By doing so we cleanse our whole emotional system and put an end to the negative relationship dynamics that fear produces in our lives. Once we acquire "power tools" to work with fear and the willful intention to do so then our lives can change profoundly for the better. We become empowered to effectively intervene in our own lives and on our own behalf. We become able to rapidly change our life results for the better in a very conscious, selective and precise manner. Gaining the power to clear fear rapidly and effectively from our lives can give us immediate relief from stress and also give us immediate improvement in our perspective, and improve our decision-making capability. In so doing we leave behind the depressed states long term fear can produce. Doing so also gives us a sense of personal empowerment that has been missing in so many people's lives. Many people have lived life fearing fear and its effects. You are not powerless in regard to fear. You can take charge of your life and release your fear, now. All that is necessary is that you make the choice.

We always make better decisions when we have first extracted fear from our emotional process. It is helpful to understand that having many fears has nothing directly to do with lacking intelligence or education; some of the most intelligent and educated people are also the most fearful. Fear can blind even the most intelligent person to their own subconscious motivations and distort their decision-making processes, without their realizing it has happened. This effect of fear leads to negative results. In fact, many highly intelligent people spend their days "thinking" what they truly believe are intelligent thoughts. In reality they are really spending their days "fearing" and projecting complex imagined negative scenarios that they have invented about what could happen in the future. All the while congratulating themselves for how intelligent they are for having done so. None of this has anything verifiably to do with what will actually happen in their future. This fear driven process is very different than using scenario thinking for constructive risk management purposes. The unfortunate mantra of many of today's CEOs is "you can never be too paranoid", what are the distortive implications on their degree of wisdom and discernment?

Fear tends to motivate us to react unconsciously, and from negative emotion, rather than to act and respond consciously and constructively, and from positive emotion or intention. Fear tends to create a very short term, and narrow view of our decisions and options in life situations. Rather than allowing us to see the true long term implications of our choices and the big picture. Therefore fear based choices are always poorer choices than choices made with wisdom, patience, and more complete information and discernment. The problem is that when we are making fear based decisions our consciousness is often so fundamentally obscured and compromised that we do not realize that the quality of our consciousness, and thus the quality of our decisions, has been diminished by fear. We often end up choosing the least fear producing option from among a list of fear producing options, rather than powerfully and creatively manifesting a situation that we consciously desire. Fear also distorts our interpretations of the results of our actions and others actions, behaviors and decisions. Therefore we could say that fear and its effects in our lives and relationships creates and represents a fundamental *learning disability* for the human species as a whole.

One main goal of this book is to empower you by giving you a method of becoming aware of your own process of fear in a way that is constructive, and which will help you effectively clear your fear from your system. We all make decisions and those of us who make decisions based upon *conscious quality values* tend to make better decisions, and thus attain better quality results. Over the course of our life time our values tend to evolve and we become "more wise" as we learn to choose better values. You could say that our values tend to shape our decisions and thus the results of our actions, and thus our lives. Therefore optimal values tend to lead to optimal results.

For many of us *fear is a value* that we often and unknowingly apply to many of our decision-making processes. However fear is a very low quality value and yields very low quality results. In fact fear often overshadows all of our other life values in our decision-making process, rendering them less meaningful in our thinking without our recognizing it as it is happening. Unfortunately fear also has the side effect of directly disrupting our decision-making processes by projecting false information into our thoughts from our imaginations. Therefore as a decision-making value fear is the worst, because it often leads us to jumping to conclusions, incorrect conclusions and making poor choices. Using fear as a key value in decision-making also often leads to self-centeredness, egoism, greed, destructive short sighted choices, interpersonal conflict, intolerance, militarism and even rationalized corruption. Globally speaking fear is also the driving force for nationalism, prejudice, war and cultural and religious intolerance in all of its most destructive forms and endemic indifference to the suffering of humanity and of the damage to the ecological environment. Some examples of higher quality values and approaches in decision-making could be wisdom, discernment, unconditional love, consciousness, tolerance, balance, compassion, patience, well-chosen life experience and being very well informed and educated. As long as fear is included in our decision-making processes these other more positive values remain unavailable, or are at least distorted or less available to us.

The approach I am taking in this book is to help you see the big picture of how fear *may have* affected all aspects of your life, so that you can fully and consciously *deconstruct* its effect and thereby arrive at fully conscious sovereign empowerment. This state of conscious sovereignty is your birthright as well as the state from which you can achieve your highest potential. No one deserves to live in fear, or to be undermined in the achievement of their dreams by fear. You deserve freedom, joy, happiness and inner peace. Those are the goals of this book and my personal goals for you. In order to accomplish these goals I discuss the nature and dynamics of fear in Chapters 1 through 5. Chapter 6 will discuss one of the most effective methods in the book for releasing fears. There are several methods to select from described in the book.

The first five chapters are designed to give you a thorough understanding of many aspects of fear so that you can make the best and most powerful use of all of the fear release techniques. From Chapter 8 onward you begin the process of working with the broader spectrum of your fears in order to facilitate you independently dismantling whatever fears and negative emotions may be influencing your life. The information included in Chapters 16 through 22 give further understanding of additional core factors that create fear dynamics, and I do suggest working with this information after learning the emotional release techniques in the book. At the back of the book in the section marked *Appendix to Chapter 8* there are four exercises that are designed to empower the reader to surface your *subconscious beliefs* and fears so that they can be worked with directly. If you are a person who is not aware of or well connected with your emotions these exercises can help you to reconnect with your deeper emotional self. We are often unaware of many of our most profoundly influential fears and beliefs and therefore they continue to detrimentally affect our lives due to our inability to focus our conscious will and healing methods on their resolution. In my work with clients I help people gradually become aware of and understand their beliefs and fears in a facilitative manner.

The exercises in the back of the book are a way of empowering the reader to become *independently self-aware* in regard to their own emotional dynamics without the help of a facilitator. This increased self-awareness can vastly improve the effectiveness of the release methods described in the book so that readers can become more effective in the management of any negative emotions they tend to feel or that affect their relationships.

In addition to releasing fears and beliefs we will also be discussing methods of releasing negative judgments, prejudices and negative emotional states of all kinds. The exercises in the Appendix can also help you to become far more aware of your emotional dynamics and relationship dynamics and thus more empowered to positively transform your life in these areas.

The great spiritual teacher Jiddu Krishnamurti, for whom I have vast respect and admiration, spoke several times on the nature of fear and on how to better understand it. I learned a great deal about fear from Krishnamurti's book "The Awakening of Intelligence". The "I am my fear" release method listed in this book was the result of some initial understandings I achieved from Krishnamurti's work and from my years of work with my clients. It took many years to develop this method of releasing fear because the method had to cover every possible type of fear a person could experience, and believe me there are many unique types of fear. It was also difficult to find a way to work directly with fear, since by our very nature human beings have an aversion to directly addressing our fears in any constructive manner.

Human beings have thousands of fears, and each one is specific to the individual, and even to the specific situation or relationship they are reacting to at the moment. I say reacting to because fear is always a process of reacting to what we are projecting in our own imaginations; it is never a reaction to what is actually happening in the moment. I will explain later what I mean by this statement. Some people have very complex fears that involve how they feel about themselves, multiple people and multiple situations. We often learn these reactive patterns of fear from others, without even realizing we have absorbed them. In order to release our fears we must have a method that is both flexible and capable of being "specifically crafted" to any unique life situation that we have been reacting to with fear, at any moment.

Another reason it was difficult to create this method was because whatever method is used must create an unavoidable "state of direct awareness and identification" with the fear we are feeling. This was necessary so that during the clearing process we cannot avoid, deny or escape the fear as we all tend to try to do when we work with our fears. *We must in some manner face our fears in order to fully transcend them.* It is this tendency to avoid, deny or try to escape our fears that keep our fears repeating over and over in our lives like a skipping record. When we avoid, suppress or deny fear, we keep the fear stuck in place in our emotional systems. The release method described in this book requires the reader to specifically identify the fear they are reacting to and in so doing to fully and permanently process it out of their system so that it is no longer "replaying" in their system. The process lets you work with your fears with such a feeling of safety that you come to clearly see your fears for what they truly are, *only an aspect of your projected imagination.* Paradoxically it is the process of fully admitting we have been carrying fear that finally allows us to permanently drop it.

Below is an "example fear" which was selected to show just how complex a fear can be, and how broad an affect it can have on one's life. This particular fear is one that I recently helped a client clear within a few minutes:

"I am afraid that if I give up my feelings of shame and my tendency to punish myself that I will then be a "bad" person. Because this will mean that I do not really care about anyone else but myself."

This person felt and had been taught that they had to feel ashamed and punish themselves in order to constantly prove that they cared for those they loved, and that if they did not do so that they did not truly care for others. This was just how they had been brought up and conditioned in their youth to show love. Of course love is not guilt or shame and these feelings are just reactive emotional expressions of the deeper fear of failing those we love and then potentially being abandoned by them for our failure. In fact feelings of guilt and shame actually inhibit us from simply, consistently and openly loving those we are close to in our lives. Our fear prevents us from realizing this simple fact.

Another example of a pervasive and complex fear I helped a client clear is:

"I am afraid that I am stupid, bad, wrong and flawed and therefore all of my choices and actions are stupid, bad, wrong and flawed, and I am afraid that there is nothing I can do to change this, and therefore I am afraid that God will never forgive me and therefore I am just screwed."

This fear covers a vast amount of territory in one's life, including one's self-image, all of one's decision-making processes, one's emotional process, and one's relationship to the divine. It also tends to lock oneself into the various fears one feels with no way out of the fears.

You could say that all fears are to a degree "self-fulfilling prophecies", since they each create such a situation of projection onto our lives that we act and make decisions *as if they are true*. Over time, this process of fear projection tends to become *a belief or set of beliefs about oneself and one's life*, which then tends to manifest in terms of one's choices and life results.

Fears can be very simple and yet in their own way be very emotionally painful as in:

"I am afraid that my husband or wife won't always find me attractive."

The fear release process you will be shown helps us realize that it is only the energy of our own imaginations that is the source of the fears we are feeling, and when we do fully accept this fact the fear releases. All that is required is that you be willing to face the initial instinctive resistance that you feel from your system when applying the method. The initial resistance is caused by your subconscious fear that is being triggered by the statement you repeat in the release process and the realization that your fear is not real or true. This resistance tends to pass very quickly. The release method described in this book for working with fear has repeatedly been shown in my sessions with clients to release or diminish their specific fears. We can release our fears or continue to live with them; it is a choice we make over and over every day. Life is better without fear.

Releasing the pain we have long buried and hidden from our conscious mind is very good for us from a self-healing standpoint. The Chapter 6 method is the "band aid off quick approach" for releasing fear. There are several other emotional release methods listed in the book. The Chapter 6 method is the most effective way I have found if you truly want to become clear of a wide variety of fears that have limited you in various areas of your life. Some people do not feel an immediate "resonance" with the method though it is powerful and effective (resonance may translate to it feeling comfortable or familiar), this is normal, no one really *enjoys* working directly with their fear, still it is necessary to process fear if you want to discard it forever. Whichever method you choose to work with I wish you success and happiness.

Chapter 1: Fear As a Part of Life:

Fear is a part of every human being's emotional life. In spite of the problems it creates in our lives it is often looked upon as a useful aspect of life because we assume that it protects us or keeps us safe from that which we fear or that which could harm us. We may also assume it keeps us safe from making "mistakes" or from repeating that which we have done in the past that we regret having done. This false rationalization is why we generally spend our lives suppressing fear, denying it, validating the need for it, trying to escape from it, trying to manage it or merely stressing over it.

Fear undermines all aspects of our lives, including our relationships, our careers and attainment of all of our life goals. Fear reduces the quality of all our mental, emotional, physical, energetic and spiritual functions. Fear is both a labyrinth and a prison of our own construction, which is for most people often subconscious, only partially perceived, and significantly misunderstood. Fear tends to paralyze us and creates indecision, internal conflict and confusion, often when we most need to be clear and decisive. Fear keeps us unnecessarily busy and wastes our energy by distracting us with our own fearful projections of what supposedly could happen, rather than allowing us to understand what is truly happening right now, so that we can take wise constructive action.

Until fear is surfaced and dealt with fully, it continues to limit us in ways we do not realize. Until we are willing to constructively explore our fears we cannot ultimately master our fears. For many of us our fears make our problems, for all intents and purposes, *undiscussible,* either with others or even in our own minds. How can we master and transcend fear if we are not even willing to own, accept and acknowledge it within ourselves or constructively discuss it between ourselves? How can we transcend it and leave it behind permanently if we do not fully understand and evaluate how it affects every area of our lives and relationships?

Because of this situation many people's lives are not everything that they want them to be or that they could be. Many people live their lives trying to survive a multitude of fears which they feel are very *real and imposing.* They may actually feel that their fears, and what they fear, "*are their lives.*" This book is designed to facilitate optimal transcendence of fears and includes methods of releasing both the energy and emotion of fear. It is my hope and intention that this information will help you to reshape your life in the manner you *consciously choose to.* I have seen this process in action and know it can be accomplished.

Fear is rooted in an amazingly simple dynamic. When we feel fear we are remembering or subconsciously referring to some *past* experience of pain, trauma or loss we have previously felt. We may also be referring to a *story* we have been told of some *potentially* painful situation that we *could* experience in the future. We then *imagine* and project onto our mind's eye a picture or movie of some similar experience or some version of that old painful experience that could occur in our future, (either to us or to someone we care about). We then see this projected picture or movie as if it were an *external physical reality* and react to it with fear. This whole process often occurs subconsciously, we simply feel the reactive feeling of fear when it is triggered. If our fears are completely subconscious they can affect our behavior and decision-making without our realizing it and keep our lives constrained and limited. In this type of situation our conscious mind remains completely unaware of our fear and we may even tell ourselves that we feel no fear at all, while our actual behavior changes to avoid what we fear. This situation can be seen when we are stuck in a comfort zone which is really a state of being imprisoned by our surrounding fears.

When we fear and we imagine potential negative futures, we are creating within our mind a vision or "holographic projection" of a future that we fear *could happen*. When we *look at the vision* which we have created in our mind's eye our body reacts with fear of that vision, because our subconscious literally does not know that the vision it is looking at is not an *external reality*. Therefore our bodies go into biological fight or flight mode and we physically stress over what we imagine. Our subconscious does not realize that what we are projecting is not actually *happening,* and that it is not a physical real world reality in our outside world. That is why we have physical stress reactions when we are afraid in a social situation, even if we do not understand exactly what it is that we fear. Because we physically feel something chemically happening *inside* our body we subconsciously believe that something "real" must be happening *outside* of ourselves. Our subconscious *actually believes* that what we fearfully project in our mind's eye *could happen or in a way is happening because it is seeing it happen.* This projection process and our emotional and biological reaction to it tend to go on unnecessarily, and endlessly, over and over.

What I am getting to with this discussion is that fear is caused by memories of unresolved past pain and trauma, many of which occurred when we were too young to truly understand what was occurring in our lives. If you had no unresolved pain or loss to project, then you would have no fear. If you have unresolved past pain and trauma you will project onto your future that it could happen again, and therefore you will fear the future reoccurrence of it. It is the resolution of the memory of our pain and trauma that we carry within our systems that resolves our fear. Fear and pain are two sides of the same coin and our healing must address both sides of the coin.

Part of the process of resolving our fear is owning our pain and trauma, which means we must also be willing to own our fear. The release processes in this book facilitate this goal. Once you have owned your pain and your fear they will be gone permanently. Until you do, you will continue to avoid them, deny them, suppress them or they will remain unhealed. This situation of leaving unhealed pain, trauma and fear unresolved is not in anyone's best interest. Especially if it leads to a deeply held yet completely unfounded fear driven tendency to believe that the pain will likely occur again in the future, and that you must therefore be ever vigilant and on guard to avoid it.

Some of you may say in response to this description, "but what happened in the past *did* happen!!! *and* I am right to fear that it could happen again!" As if that makes your memory of what happened in the past "real" in the present moment and therefore to be feared. To this statement I would respond with the following. Yes, of course whatever happened that caused your pain, trauma or loss in the past did happen; at least as you remember it. Yes you did record a memory of what happened, and depending upon how terrible it was you may have "seared it deeply into your emotional system". Yes you are also replaying a memory of it and projecting that memory onto your mind's eye in the present. Yes you are projecting it into your future in your imagination, and then you are reacting with fear to this projection of memory and imagination. Still I would say that you do not actually fear what happened in the past; you fear what you are *projecting from your memory of what happened* in the past onto your mind's eye *in the present*. You fear what the past situation tells your mind, via your imagination, could happen in the present or in your future.

You need not have your present or future emotional state, relationships, life choices or options dictated by unresolved or incompletely processed memories and traumas from your past. Nor does your future have to be limited by imagined fears of what could happen. Your fear need not define your decisions or your options for you. You also need not have your perceived identity or self-image be limited by your fear, or worse *become your fear*. You can transcend the past and learn to live fully and consciously in the present, and this is my hope for you.

A concrete example of how this projection process works would be the following. Imagine you are being chased by a tiger through the jungle and the tiger running is only ten seconds behind you. You are very frightened in this situation. Oddly enough you are not really scared of the tiger; you are actually scared of what you subconsciously imagine the tiger will do to you *ten seconds in the future if it catches you and eats you.* This is a vital distinction, in that it is not actually the physical reality of the presence of tiger you are reacting to, it is your own projected, imagined picture of the tiger's capacity to hurt you that you are reacting to. That is what you are actually afraid of. This is a crucial distinction and understanding, and a very different way of looking at your situation and at life. It tells much about how our systems manage information we process and how we perceive and process our experience of *time*.

The prior paragraph was a *reinterpretation* of the experience of fear that most people experience. This process of re-interpreting and re-understanding life situations and how we experience fear within them is fundamental. Once you understand fear in this new way you will realize that you are not actually afraid of anything outside of yourself. What you are afraid of is only what you have created and imagined *within yourself.* In fact you have therefore only ever been afraid of yourself! You have taken your interpretation of the external situation and added your own imagining of what *could happen*, to the vision you created in your mind's eye.

Through this example of the tiger we can arrive at the key understanding that we are never really afraid of any external reality, event, situation or person in the present moment. We are only afraid of the internal picture or movie that we have created in our mind's eye. What we are really afraid of has no absolute basis in fact or reality whatsoever, and is solely a creation of our own mental and emotional system. Therefore we can say in the most absolute sense that what we all fear is only and absolutely our own imagined creations. Once you fully realize this you will no longer fear your fears any more than you would fear holding your own hand up in front of your face.

When we create these projected negative imaginings we assume that we are helping and protecting ourselves in some way from what we imagine could happen. We even assume that being afraid of what we imagine will keep us safe from what we imagine. In reality the opposite is the case. In fact doing so gives energy to what we fear and can inadvertently work *to manifest what we fear in our lives.* In addition the fear that we hold onto paralyzes and limits us and distorts and obscures our view of how powerful we really are in every present moment. Fear magnifies our life and relationship problems and perceived obstacles while diminishing our awareness of our true ability to effectively deal with them. Fear drains our energy and triggers us into a variety of negative emotional states just when we need to be energetic, courageous, positive, strong, focused and intentional. Fear distracts us from the key priorities that are most important for us to focus on and mires us in illusion, false interpretations and unimportant details. Fear blinds us to the many creative options we really have available to us in every moment of our lives to positively manifest a better reality.

Our fears keep us focused on avoidance of negative future potentials, rather than focusing on creating what we want. In truth fear neither solves nor achieves anything, whereas conscious awareness, determination and intention does. For those readers who esteem to achieve inner peace it is important to realize that we cannot have inner mental, emotional or spiritual peace and also be in a state of fear of anything at the same time. Fear must first go if we want to be at peace, to feel complete joy, to live in love, and to be truly happy.

The Human System of Fears Affects All Levels of Humanity:
Most individual human beings have developed a subconscious system or framework of *thousands* of projected fears that they unconsciously *try to use* to motivate themselves to overcome life's adversities. They also try to use these fears to "navigate their lives" in terms of making decisions by constantly trying to avoid what they fear rather than by positively and constructively working toward their conscious goals. For many of us this system of interwoven subconscious fears has become the core of our life decision-making strategies. Unfortunately most of us do not realize this process is even going on and therefore its effects occur without our awareness or effective ability to intervene on our own behalf.

Thus our personal *system of fears* is largely transparent to us, even as we live within it, almost like an invisible movable prison of life limitations. Each of our individual systems of fears tends to change over time as we each grow older, learn more about life, relationships and ourselves and we each evolve. The fears that you hold as a middle aged person are usually very different than the fears you held as a teenager. The system of fears that you will die with as an old person will likely be very different than the system of fears that you had as a middle aged person or the fears you had as a child. In effect you learn to fear more things as you age and you learn to fear different things. The supposed value of believing in and holding onto our fears is constantly being reinforced by those we are in relationship with and by society in general. We are constantly told by others that our fears are necessary to keep us safe and supposedly necessary to empower and to keep us in control of our lives. I have had multiple clients ask me "should I be afraid of this situation" or "I do not know if I should be afraid". Of course there is no situation we "should" be afraid or that can be better dealt with by applying fear.

In effect we learn to fear new situations and things from others, therefore you could say that fear "catches like a virus" from one person to another. We can catch fears from friends, family or even from watching a news show on television. Some people and even organizations intentionally "breed new fears" and communicate them in order to affect people's decision-making, and thereby to herd large groups of people like cattle. Less astute or evolved politicians sometimes operate this way. Unfortunately today's mass telecommunications systems support this process far more effectively than past systems of communication and it appears that it is creating a more general tendency to resonate with fear in the general population.

The assumption that fear empowers us in any way is false and misleading. Our fears only disempower and mislead us, distorting our interpretations of our experiences and tainting our decision-making. Our fears also distort our interpretations of the results of our actions and other's actions. Still it is important to realize that not only individuals are affected by fear, the decision-making processes of groups of all kinds (all of which are made up of individuals) are also heavily impacted by fear energies and fear dynamics.

What is also not realized is that there is a *larger system of fears* that much of the *collective consciousness* of all of the people who inhabit the planet has tended to function within, and which has limited the development of our species as a whole. The collective consciousness system of fears is constantly referenced by most human beings in their group decision-making processes, though they are mostly unconscious of this process. These group decision-making processes function at the level of small teams, at the level of large groups, at the level of international corporations, at the level of religious institutions, and even at the level of governments and whole nations of people. This process can be seen to be at work in situations of war and nationalism.

The effect of these systems of fear undermines the quality of decision-making and the quality of interpretive consciousness exhibited by all of these groups constantly. These fear driven intergroup dynamics lead to ongoing judgmentalness, anger, hatred, competition, fear reactions of all kinds and even poisonous multi-generational resentment between rival groups and nations. This process of fear based limitation of thought, emotion, consciousness and decision-making has caused significant global misunderstandings, international conflict, distrust, fear between nations, wars, and made international cooperative efforts and teamwork very difficult.

This globally maladaptive situation of course must change soon for the good of all. Our current tenuous global circumstances of high populations, low food production, low energy resources, high potentials for rapid spread of disease, spread of terrorism, global warming, etc. cannot allow us to continue to operate in this dysfunctional, distrustful and fear bound manner. When we learn as individuals to operate independently from the influence of this larger collective fear based mindset we become sovereign in our ability to creatively manifest our future and to attain consistent happiness. It is crucial for the future of our world that more and more individuals wake up to their potential to live fearless lives, sovereignly independent from the fear based dynamics and beliefs of their cultures, religions, political systems and familial conditioning. Freeing individuals to live in freedom from fear of all kinds, whether it is their own internal fear or the fears that are existent in their surrounding community is a key goal of this book.

For individuals, our tendency to project fear in our own emotional systems is one main reason that positive affirmations and other systems of manifesting what we want in life do not work effectively. It is also why many systems of self-transformation that are taught today do not work more effectively. Meaning that these techniques are working *against or in direct opposition to* the complex and pervasively internalized patterns and strategies of unconscious fear that are so deeply entrenched in our systems. They are working against our system of fears, without taking our system of fears directly into account, nor directly addressing our fears, nor resolving our fears in a constructive and decisive manner. Therefore, when we apply any system of positive self-transformation or change we are actually to a degree *fighting our own primal self-protective instincts*. Many of these systems actually see working with fears directly as not being "positive enough" or focusing exclusively on the positive. In so doing they lose the capacity to face and transcend the fact of deeply rooted negative subconscious dynamics and emotions which will not go away simply because we hold a positive conscious mind set.

This fear projection tendency and process is also why there is unresolved conflict in the larger world around us and even within nations. One example would be in the United States Government, between the Democrats and Republicans, where the fear that each party has of the other's power to assume control has closed down communications and thus the potential for negotiations and progress. Until the fear that political parties and nations have for each other is admitted and acknowledged, and then addressed and transcended in some effective manner, it is impossible for there to be effective discussion and resolution. Right now the U.S. Government is caught in a *gridlock of fear*, and it does not understand that this is the truth of the situation and is therefore unwilling to recognize it, admit it and effectively deal with it. No one wants to admit how fearful and vulnerable they feel because they may then be perceived weak, incompetent or ineffectual. Fear is human, not a sign of incompetence.

For many people fear gridlock has fully paralyzed their lives, and they have become unable to change anything in their lives significantly for the better. Many people's usual way of making a decision is to let one fear that they *fear more* than any other fear be their decision-making criteria and motivation for change. For example they decide to stay in a bad relationship because they *fear more* being alone, or they believe that no one else will want them. For many of us it is only when a "trumping fear" occurs in our lives that real change becomes possible, as in a crisis situation. This is true also of how change occurs in large corporations and even in nations.

Our fears define the parameters of what we politely call our "comfort zone". We tend to remain within our cage of fears and try to make the best of it, while our life slowly deteriorates in some fundamental ways. Eventually something *significantly more fear producing* happens and we are driven past our other fears to make fundamental changes in our lives. The trumping fear producing situation may be terrifying, yet it may also bring fundamental and constructive change to our lives. We may not realize until long afterward how beneficial these changes were, if we ever do. My suggestion is to release your fears now, today! Don't wait for fear to make your decisions for you. Expand your vision and your options by clearing your fears as fast as you can so that you no longer make your decisions as merely the result of reactions to your fears. Make your decisions based on deep self-awareness of who you are and what you want, and by acquiring quality information that you can constructively use to create the life you really want. If any fears are triggered on the path to creating what you want, release them and keep going.

Fears Become Negative Beliefs:
For many people the process of projecting energy into their fears has been going on for so long and so intensely that their fears have actually become beliefs about their lives and about who they are as a person! For example if a person has feared for a long time that no one would

ever love them, they then begin to think these thoughts over and over, then they may start to actually *believe* that no one ever will. Once we choose to believe something to be true we then begin to *act, behave and make decisions* as if it was a fact. This tendency to act and make decisions based upon what we *fear to be true*, rather than what we *know to be true*, is how we then manifest or create what we most fear in our lives. It is important that we understand how fears relate to our beliefs, and how our beliefs drive our actions, and how our actions create our life experiences and results. This process of what we fear being created in our lives can be seen most often and clearly in our relationships. It is quite common for fear of abandonment driven jealousy and mistrust to drive couples to become angry, hateful, and controlling and in so doing to tear their relationships apart.

Fear can be a very destructive element in your life if it becomes *the default method by which you choose to create what you believe* about yourself, your life, your relationships, other people or the world. It is not a big step to go from fearing yourself to be a "bad" person to actually *believing* it. It is not a big step to go from fearing that others *may be* bad people to *believing* that they are bad people. This is a serious issue and process worth contemplating and understanding. What we believe about the world, we tend to project *onto* the world and then to manifest or create in our lives. This means that in the long run, whatever you choose to believe about yourself and the world you may then experience, even if it is not really true, beneficial or healthy to do so. It also means that you can only release core fear related beliefs by first recognizing and then *releasing the associated fear* that holds them to be in place in your emotional system.

If your fears create many of your beliefs, then they can create much of what you perceive to be your *reality*. All of our beliefs, whether fear based or not, become *projections onto our experienced reality* and thus distort our experience of what is really happening in our lives from moment-to-moment. All beliefs are filters on our experience of life. This process of distorting our reality by projecting what we *choose to believe* about life, others and ourselves need not be the case, we can simply learn to see and experience what truly factually is, in the moment, without filters. Still most people currently know of no other way to create how they see life or how they make the decisions that create their life results.

Subconscious fears and fear based beliefs also tend to create what could be looked at as *two dimensional thinking* and views of reality, or in simple terms a tendency toward "if this happens, then that will happen, style thinking". This type of thinking tends to create self-sabotaging internal dialog that then affects our decisions and our performance in achieving our goals in life. For example, when we have fears of social rejection or fears of failure we may often have internal dialog or "self-talk" that can go something like this:

- "If I try to make new friends I will probably end up making a fool of myself"
- "If I ask the girl out that I am attracted to she will probably tell me she already has a boyfriend"
- "If I try online dating then all the men I attract will be *players* and none of them will want a serious committed relationship"
- "If I try to achieve my goals I will probably put out a huge amount of effort and feel terrible about wasting my time when I fail"
- "If I try to achieve my goals I will just fail like I always do"

These types of thought patterns and internal dialog are created by subconscious projections of feared negative future outcomes. They can be significantly debilitating if we do not recognize what is creating them. They are *false and misleading* thoughts and are only projections of our subconscious fears. These thoughts and their influence can be transcended by releasing the fears that drive the negative thoughts. Life is not two dimensional, it is far more complex and beautiful and far more full of potential, and we ourselves are far more creative and capable of achieving our goals than we often realize, feel, tell ourselves or think. "If this then that thinking" only manifests limitation and a narrow view of our options and potential. I would suggest becoming very consciously aware of whatever you tend to tell yourself about yourself, your life and relationships from now on.

Your fears are constantly going on below the level of your conscious awareness, and *to a degree* are constantly creating your experienced reality without your understanding that this is happening. Is this the way you want to create your life? I am not trying to raise or trigger your fears by saying these statements. My intention in this book is to raise your conscious awareness of how your fears *can* affect your life and *can* undermine your conscious awareness, and *can* affect your decisions. When you clear your fears they will no longer limit nor diminish your power or your happiness. When you clear your fears you can be free to live life as you sovereignly and joyfully choose to.

Fear based beliefs are generally subconscious and often go unquestioned as to their validity or usefulness in our lives, so we do not tend to find motivation to cleanse them from our systems. Once our fears have created fear based beliefs, those fear based beliefs tend to generate fear based *repetitive thoughts and internal dialog* on a daily basis. Our fear based thoughts then tend to directly influence our daily life decisions. Once our decisions are influenced by our fear based thoughts then our life results and relationships are directly affected to our detriment. This ongoing influence of our fears, our fearful beliefs and resulting fearful thoughts and their effect on our decisions has an ongoing and *cumulative effect* across our lifetime. This ongoing dynamic takes us away from our consciously desired goals and dreams without our realizing that it is happening. We think that we are avoiding problems, while we are actually avoiding positively working toward and accomplishing our goals. This all occurs without our realizing that the *real problem* is that we're in fear to begin with, and that our decision-making process has been somewhat compromised and undermined by fear at subconscious levels. This happens to individuals, to the consciousness of large groups and even to the consciousness of nations. This detrimental process undermines the possibility of creating positive, loving and creative results in all areas of life and at all levels of society around the world.

Right now there are nations and cultures that are holding onto fear and making decisions from a place of projected fear and distrust based upon remembered past pain and trauma. They focus on and work in these detrimental directions without realizing that they could instead be building bridges of trust, teamwork and collaboration with other nations and cultures. Until we all choose to heal and release our fear and pain and let go of the past, as individuals and as nations, we cannot move forward to create a peaceful world.

Optimism and Being Positive Are Not Enough:
I find that having a positive and optimistic approach in general to life is essential. It is also good to regularly state positive affirmations and to be willing to make bold positive empowered choices and actions toward goals you have clearly thought through. Still we cannot ignore our process of fear and its effects. It is also necessary to understand that when we do state positive affirmations and initiate bold choices we tend to unknowingly *trigger our underlying fears*, which simultaneously resist our best positive attempts to change ourselves and our lives for the better. Our fears are triggered because when we make bold positive choices and actions we are *initiating change* in our lives and we all have some fear of these changes. So in order to make significant progress in life without incurring internal emotional conflict we must first resolve our fears.

One powerful benefit I have found from the release method in this book is that once you have identified your fears, working with this method tends to release aspects of *other* fears you did not even know you had. In effect the technique surfaces new insights and understandings into your emotional process. By opening your mind to understanding the various other fears that you did not realize you have been holding and working upon, you are empowered to rapidly release and thus free yourself from them. This process is catalytic, in that it speeds your self-transformation and consciousness development faster than you may have realized it could occur. In effect over time you cease to be distracted by fear projections and become free to focus on more beneficial and constructive thought processes.

I do respect all life transformation methods and emotional release methods that are available today; I suggest they can be utilized *in conjunction* with the methods listed in this book and thus their effect can be optimized and enhanced. There are several other emotional release techniques such as:

- EMDR (Eye Movement Desensitization and Reprocessing)
- Hypnosis
- The Sedona Method
- The Hawaiian healing technique called the Ho' Oponopono
- EFT (The Emotional Freedom Technique) often referred to as "Tapping"
- Prayer of all kinds
- Sanskrit Mantras which are very powerful and flexible methods of working with fear and other negative emotions, as well as tools for working with any other life problem or toward any spiritual attainment

Other life management techniques which usually require regular daily practice to achieve optimal results, such as Mindfulness Meditation, Yoga, Qi Gong and Tai Chi can be very helpful if utilized over the long term. One of my favorite emotional release techniques, which is very generally applicable to resolving negative emotional issues, is briefly described in a book called the "Untethered Soul: The Journey Beyond Yourself" by Michael A. Singer.

There is a highly developed method of self-transformation called NLP (Neurolinguistic Programming) which is very powerful. In very wise, experienced and intuitively guided hands NLP can be helpful. Unfortunately it also has the potential to be profoundly misused and misapplied. You could now find its influence in high level executive manipulative management practices, hard core political advertising and in various kinds of sales and product marketing. NLP can be used to very subtly use language, whether verbally spoken or in written form, to directly and subconsciously affect how people think, feel, interpret situations and events, and therefore make decisions. Therefore although I do suggest NLP as a viable option to those seeking to release fears, I also suggest careful evaluation of practitioner's integrity and reputation and careful thought as to your personal goals, prior to seeking this type of facilitation.

It is important to understand the ongoing state of dynamic tension created when we focus on positive affirmations and intentions when we also have pre-existing subconscious fears working in opposition to our conscious goals. A practical example of this dynamic is seen in the fear reaction that we fight every time we choose to go on a diet. We decide that we want to change our weight for the better and our system reacts with a variety of fears of doing so. This can create a fearful tug of war between our currently perceived identity, which we fear losing or changing in any way, (we all fear change) and the new self or perceived identity we want to create and fear changing into. We also fear the pain of not eating the preferred foods we like, the discomfort of changing our daily routine, the pain of not eating as much as we want to eat, and we fear not having the emotional comfort we derive from eating comfort foods. If however we first release all our fears of going on the diet then it becomes much easier to diet. If any other fears or insecurities arise *while* we diet they can be released immediately and continuing on the diet becomes far more feasible. We may even fear what will happen after we have lost weight, as in fearing being more attractive and facing the dating scene and the potential for relationship rejection or abandonment. These fears can also be released preemptively.

When any necessary life change (whether perceived to be positive or negative) is looked at *without fear* we become far more empowered to affect it in our lives. Therefore we get better results and faster results and these results tend to stay with us. If we fear "falling off the wagon" on our diet, then that fear causes even more stress, which then causes us to seek food to comfort us, which then causes us to fall off the diet wagon. Again the answer is to clear the fear before beginning the diet process, and once we have no fears then the dieting process works better. Then we can maintain the diet because we do not fear failing ourselves or others. The same is true of breaking any addiction. If we fear falling off the wagon in regard to alcohol, drugs, sex or any other type of addiction we will tend to seek that which we are addicted to in order to manage the fear and stress. Releasing these fears of breaking the addiction reduces the desire for the addictive substance.

We often do not know we have fears because we do not want to know we have them, or because they were created and conditioned into us in our early youth, and are thus subconscious, and therefore affect us subconsciously. We may even have fears because we have been taught by our parents or society that they are "good fears" for us to have. We may have been taught that it is "smart" to be afraid and to interpret, to decide and to act in fear. We may have been taught that acting out socially in fear driven anger is a sign of being "powerful" and thus of being safe, respectable, and thus more secure and thus less likely to be socially abandoned. Since everyone around us functions this same way we continue to assume that this is normal, natural, wise and necessary, although it is completely maladaptive and creates chaos in our lives and relationships. At heart humans are herd creatures and functioning like the rest of the herd is expected behavior.

Our "systems and strategies of fear" keep us limited and unconscious of key aspects of our lives and our own process of powerfully creating our lives. Like the story of Gulliver who was tied down by the tiny Lilliputians, we are each tied down by hundreds or even thousands of our own minor or major subconscious fears. Unless each fear is cleared from our systems, they will continue to imprison us and limit our consciousness and our future options. Whether they are the fears of abandonment, criticism, death, illness, being betrayed, not being good enough, failure, change, the unknown, conflict, not being liked or any of a thousand other fears. They all limit us from taking direct intelligent empowered constructive action on our own behalf, right now.

Most of us are afraid of facing our fears directly, and oddly enough of thus releasing and transcending our fears. This is because making decisions completely without fear is an *unknown situation* for most people. Most of us have no idea what living life free from fear would be like, thus this potential triggers our fear of the unknown. We also fear being different from other people in this fundamental way, even though it is so very good for us to live fearlessly. We fear standing out from the crowd in this fundamental and fearless way. I am drawing a distinction here between acting truly fearlessly and acting in an arrogant, pushy, bullying and condescending manner. These tendencies are representative of fear, not representations of fearlessness. People who act this way are simply more afraid of not being aggressive and of thus appearing weak and vulnerable than they are brave or fearless.

Up until now, in human history fear has actually acted as a useful set of "training wheels" on most human being's decision-making processes. We have tended to try to use our fears to hold us back from hurting ourselves, and those we care about when we make decisions, take actions and express our emotions. Until we learn as individuals and as a species to develop conscious discipline, discernment and emotional self-management methods we will continue to depend upon fear to "give us pause" and to repress our even more maladaptive emotions. This desirable management of our decision-making process can be accomplished far better via discernment, wisdom and conscious intentional decision-making design than by fear.

Many of us feel that we lack and require more self-confidence, self-esteem or self-worth and strive to develop these traits. In fact it is more often the case that we have a deep fear of what would happen socially or interpersonally if we took action on our own behalf, or we fear that we are not good enough to do so, or we fear that we will make a mistake. Ultimately we fear hurting ourselves or others through misuse of our decision-making power or influence. Having a deep fear is a very different situation than *lacking* self-worth or self-confidence. If we are not self-aware enough to realize we have a fear or are unwilling to acknowledge that we have a fear we may not be able to tell the difference, and thus may not be able to apply the proper solution to our situation. Confidence and self-worth building exercises alone are not an antidote to fear. If we have fears and we try to build our confidence our fears simply drain away our confidence without our realizing why or how it is happening. Once our fears are cleared, affirmations for confidence and self-worth building tend to work quite easily and without internal resistance. Until our fears are released they tend to sap our confidence and feelings of self-worth.

I am not suggesting that fear itself is actually a problem; in the distant past humans needed to be able to "run away from bears", and the emotion of fear triggered adrenalin, and therefore could help to save us from some rare situations. That said, fear has now become a maladaptive emotion in our rapidly changing, highly technologized and increasingly socially and politically complex world. It is now a source of distorted consciousness, misinterpretation of reality, projection of false future probabilities, confusion, anxiety, stress, conflict, disunity, war and unwise competition. Fearful interpretive processes and decision-making are just a developmental phase on humanities path to greater conscious awareness, both as individuals and as a species. I am suggesting that all of us can move through this developmental phase more quickly, efficiently and effectively than most of us currently do. I am also suggesting that this specific evolution of consciousness which transcends fear is necessary for the world as a whole to progress without unnecessary global destructiveness and violence.

I do not suggest that human beings focus on developing self-control, because self-control is a process of emotional self-suppression, which is unhealthy and ultimately self-defeating. Self-control is a process of disassociating oneself from what we feel rather than embracing what we feel and constructively managing it in the most optimal and opportune way. Self-Control creates a battle within oneself between two or more conflicted parts of oneself, which creates internal stress, disunity, disharmony and therefore does not support inner peace. Self-control cannot result in self-love, unconditional love of others, compassion or inner peace. Negative emotions will always find some way to covertly and detrimentally express themselves and often remain unconscious as they do. Self-control in the absolute sense is simply not achievable, whereas mental and emotional *self-management* is achievable and can constantly be refined and evolved. Many people want control of their lives and chase after it endlessly, yet it can never be achieved and chasing it is a waste of time and only creates more problems, both in their relationships and within their own emotional process. On the flip side of the emotional process, speaking from the vantage point of positive emotions, most of us certainly would not want to "control or limit" how much love, joy, inner peace and happiness we feel.

There is nothing in life that we can *absolutely control* for any length of time, although our fears drive us endlessly to want to assert control and to believe that it is possible so that we can feel "safe and powerful". This is especially true in regard to our relationships, our financial security and our physical and emotional safety. None of us have absolute control over anything in our lives nor ever can we have. We all do however have *some* power and *some* influence in the world and if we use it consciously and intelligently we can leverage it effectively to create the lives we want. Doing so without fear creates the optimal situation for all of us. If we taint our creative process with fear we then misuse our power and influence and create chaos and problems for ourselves and others. If we try to control in the name of safety, rationalizing that it is possible or even good, we create more problems that we solve.

Fear in relationships can wear the false guise of "caring". This is true because in relationships we are often taught that if we do not fear for those we love that we do not *really* care for and love them. This is neither true nor healthy and actually uses precious mental and emotional energy in *fearing* which could be better used in *loving* and in taking constructive intelligent action for those we love in the present. We need not fear in order to take good care of those we love. Fear driven decisions in relationships of course represent codependent dynamics. It is often true that people we are in relationship with want us to empathize with, and resonate with, their fears. They literally want us to "fear along with them", in order to prove to them that we care and to help them feel safer. Unfortunately they may not realize that by dragging others into their fear states they are only creating an expanded social emotional dysfunction, rather than decisively resolving their problems. If we allow ourselves to be subconsciously triggered and entrained into this type emotional dynamic we can easily become lost in it to our detriment and also to the detriment of those we love. I am not suggesting being insensitive to people in fear states, I am suggesting that sharing fear states and resonating with them is a detrimental practice. Fear does not equal love, nor does control equal love. There are useful times to be empathetic and non-useful times.

Fear as the Root of Negative Emotion and Ego:

As stated earlier it is my assertion and observation that fear is the root of every negative emotional state, whether it be anger, hatred, jealousy, depression, resentment, guilt, shame, or believe it or not, even sadness. If we can find within ourselves the *root fear* associated with our current negative emotional state and directly release that fear, then the associated negative emotional state will collapse like a house of cards. An example of this process would be when we hate someone we feel is trying to undermine us at work and get us fired and thereby potentially threaten our families' financial wellbeing. We hate them because we fear the negative potential future situation it appears that they could have the power to create. If we clear the fear we feel for our family's wellbeing and our own wellbeing then the associated hatred immediately disappears. I am not suggesting not caring that someone is trying to undermine us at work. I am suggesting that we can probably handle the situation much better if we are neither afraid nor hating another person while we are consciously, rationally and effectively addressing the detrimental situation. We will be far more creatively effective in our capacity to develop a solution to the problem if we are neither afraid nor busy trying to destroy the other person. I say destroy because the emotion of hatred is in truth the desire to destroy that which we hate; I will explain what I mean by this statement.

Hatred is actually a complex and misunderstood emotion and is an intense primal defensive fear reaction. It is made up of five parts. First is the feeling of powerlessness. Second is the feeling of vulnerability. Third is the feeling of anger. Fourth is a specific judgment or blame of someone or something that we see as the threat that we feel so vulnerable to and so powerless in regard to. The fifth and last element of hatred is the desire to destroy that which we feel so vulnerable to and threatened by. Our primal-self feels so profoundly threatened that it sees no other solution to our situation other than to destroy the perceived threat. Therefore hatred is nothing more than our *most intense fear reaction*. Destroying/hating someone else is the second most extreme *form of trying to control* that we can *attempt to apply* to another human being. Killing is the *most extreme* form of trying to control another person.

Hatred is of course always a misguided emotion. Still we must understand the true nature of and rationalization behind hatred if we want to effectively resolve, heal and transcend it forever. Hatred is an extreme reaction to our own perceived victimhood and it creates a desire to control the perceived victimizer! *Thus hatred stems from the mindset (whether "real" or completely illusionary), of our perceived victimhood.* In later chapters *t*his understanding of hatred will prove to be pivotal in learning to deal with fear and hatred, whether it is our own hatred or hatred we perceive in the emotional systems of others. Supposedly, if we have destroyed (killed or fundamentally diminished in power) another person through acts of hatred, we have then completely "controlled them". Obviously most of us do not kill those we hate, though often in some part of ourselves we may desire to or we may wish that we could. We tend to hide these deeper primal destructive desires from others, and even from our own conscious minds.

This definition of what hatred actually is has profound implications when we think of what are commonly referred to today as "hate crimes and hate speech". Hate crimes are punished more severely than other types of crimes and are often seen as more heinous than other crimes and even as "evil". I would suggest that those who perpetrate these types of crimes are actually motivated at subconscious levels by deep seated unreconciled fears, feelings of powerlessness and vulnerability, and that they are using their destructive acts and words as a way of proving to themselves and others that they have control over the world and their lives. If it is truly fear that drives hatred, can we destroy hatred by punishing it away? Can we destroy the fear in a fearful person by making them even more afraid of the power of authority and of being punished? Can we destroy their hatred by creating an even greater fear in them that we may destroy them? Is it actually wrong for a human being to be so afraid that they could hate, or is it simply a sign of a deep social or personal dysfunction that needs to be constructively and preemptively addressed? I think we can do better if we only choose to try.

I feel that there is a need for a deeper understanding of this most destructive human dynamic which we call hatred that can truly bring constructive proactive solutions, rather than simply aggravating the existing problem through blindly and hatefully punishing it after the fact. If you further take away the power and feeling of control that a fearful and hateful person has by punishing them, do you not simply breed further hatred in them? Won't they someday get out of prison? Will their hatred not potentially show up in some other area of their lives or live on in their children? I am not suggesting not dealing effectively with the problem of hatred; I am suggesting using far more sophisticated and effective tools than simple blunt force punishment and imprisonment to try to solve this complex problem. We cannot legislate fear and hatred away, police it away, kill it away, ignore it away, or hate it away. Fear and hatred can only be resolved through investing in each other and teaching each other and creating conscious understanding, educated perspective, mutual trust, respect, forgiveness and unconditional love. Unless we are willing to place these as our priorities fear and hatred will go on endlessly.

Hatred is our most primal and last ditch effort to protect ourselves from that which we so intensely fear. Please remember these words, hatred begets hatred. Meaning hatred is a reactive and reflexive process, like a knee jerk reaction when your knee is tapped by a doctor's hammer. When we feel that we are hated we tend to reflexively and defensively hate because we feel so vulnerable and powerless to other's hatred. When we hate others they feel it and they tend to reflexively hate us. The same is true of fear and mistrust. Meaning that when we fear mistrust others they feel our fear and mistrust and in turn tend to reactively and instinctively fear mistrust us. If they fear and mistrust us we instinctively fear and mistrust them. These reactive emotional processes go on at subconscious levels between people every day without our realizing it. Few people are conscious enough to recognize them and then apply effective methods to transcend their effects, and by doing so avoid their corrosive and detrimental influences on even our most basic day-to-day decision-making. The negative problems and results we see around the world are evidence of this vicious cycle. Fear and hatred create misunderstanding, distrust, assumptions of negative intent on the part of those we mistrust, and conflict and aggression, which then create more of the same.

On a global scale many of us are currently fearing and hating and trying to destroy terrorists. These terrorists hate the western world and any other people who do not agree with or share their extreme beliefs. The more we fear and hate the terrorists and choose to kill and destroy them the more hateful terrorists we tend to create from the residual global population. Hatred only breeds more hatred, whether it is them hating us or us hating them. We need more conscious and sophisticated means of dealing with terrorism than merely fighting and killing, and it is clear that governments are just now realizing this fact and taking some initial action in this direction. War is no longer a viable means of solving problems in a world where all nations are economically, politically and technologically dependent upon all other nations. Technology and science alone will not solve our global emotional problems. If we can find a way to remove fear from the mix *on all sides* then perhaps communication, understanding, negotiation and ultimately peaceful resolution will become possible. This could then lead to far more global collaboration and teamwork than is currently being demonstrated, which is sorely needed if we want to build a better world.

Everyone has an ego and egos run on desire and fear. We desire life, time, money, recognition, love, sex, power, control, security, safety, etc.. Often our motivations for what we desire are not merely for pleasure, though we often do not realize it. Quite often we desire what we desire because we unknowingly assume our desires will *help us manage our fears and stress.* It is important to consciously understand the relationship between our desires and our fears. This is why wherever we have a significant desire for *anything* there will be a fear of either not having what we desire, not getting what we desire or of losing what we desire. Whether the fear we feel is the fear of death or abandonment, of embarrassment, of not having a desired relationship, of being alone, of not having enough of what we want, of not being deserving of what we want or fear of the challenges associated with getting what we want.

Egos are an outgrowth of the subconscious and in large part are a *self-defense mechanism* against being hurt by others socially, emotionally and interpersonally as we proceed through life and strive to manifest what we desire or choose. Meaning that our "systems of fear" are the part of our egos that hold us back from acting in an *overly confident* manner or from following our blind primal desires to our detriment. Therefore our systems of fear tend to keep us from making unwise decisions without thinking and without caring about the implications or consequences of our actions. Meaning that until we become *conscious enough* of how to make wise and discerning decisions we continue to depend upon our fears to motivate us to "look before we leap" in various areas of life and relationships. We simultaneously depend upon our fears to motivate us to take action on our own behalf to protect ourselves and those we love. This fear driven decision-making process in human beings cannot continue as it has, it costs far more than it is worth. The destructive aspects of it are too numerous to count and it tends to keep people from becoming more conscious of their actions rather than waking them up to conscious self-accountability and recognizing the long term implications of their choices.

The process of shifting from making decisions based on fear to making decisions based upon conscious understanding and discerning wisdom is in part dependent upon how long we have lived (time), life experiences and the quality of education we have access to and is also a process of dissolving the ego. It is also necessary to release the fear that drives the whole egoic process; otherwise the ego will continue to strive to control our interpretations of life and our decisions. We cannot be wise and egotistical at the same time. We cannot be wise and fearful at the same time. The ego, and with it, much of what we refer to as our personality and perceived identity, is only a self-defense mechanism created by the subconscious to keep itself safe from its fear of the world, death, loss of control, rejection and abandonment.

Most of us are so identified with the various aspects of our personalities that we have come to believe that our ego, our personality, the beliefs we took on subconsciously growing up and even our often negative reactive emotions and behaviors are "just who we are". Our negative emotions are not who we are, they are not our identity; they need never define us or our relationships, nor become our reality. They need never define or limit our way of life, or relationships, nor our future. It is only through deep introspection and through releasing the fears that bind us that we can realize that there is far more to us than our egos.

It is better to make decisions without ego and without fear, since both ego and fear cloud our process of clearly and cleanly learning from our life experience and our decisions. Both create a straight-jacket on the process of attaining conscious understanding and of feeling unconditional love for self and others. It is very important to realize that many people have unknowingly and subconsciously been taught to use fear not only as their main *decision-making criteria and value* in life, but as their *main motivational emotion* in life. While they are in subconscious fear they are consciously calling themselves streetwise, smart, cautious, "intelligent skeptics", logical, scientifically minded or even incredible to say more "rational" than others. Without realizing it they are often so "mind focused" that their consciousness has become very *disassociated* from their own emotional fear process altogether, even while it runs their system. Meaning they can no longer feel their own fear, therefore they cannot assess its influence on their decisions, mindset or mental processes. This situation is truly detrimental if you want to live a life of joy and happiness. How can you consistently feel and experience your joy, love and happiness if you are only in your mind? The process of mere thought, logic and analytical thinking is not a process of loving emotion, though these mental processes are lately lauded as the highest form of function in many societies. Thought and joy are mutually exclusive states. Thought and love are mutually exclusive states. I am not suggesting deleting thought from life, I am suggesting understanding how you create your thoughts and consciously and intelligently managing the process. I am also suggesting prioritizing love and thought wisely in your process of life decision-making. You can accomplish this through developing conscious discernment.

Living in one's mind is ultimately an empty state, though some may see it as empowering because they fear the influence of their own emotions on their decisions because they fear that their emotions will create unwanted vulnerability. (Later in this book we will describe why *conscious emotional vulnerability* is your most powerful state of consciousness.)

Living only in one's mind literally creates another form of learning disability for those who function this way, in that it creates an inability to learn from our own emotional process and our emotional experience of life. It also creates an inability to share the emotional world that others are experiencing. Certainly there are plenty of negative emotions in the world that others are feeling and acting upon that I do not suggest sharing with others. I do suggest helping others manage their negative emotions, and doing so does involve some small degree of empathetic emotional sharing. However if we are constantly stuck in our minds, we become unable to share with others the joyful, loving and exhilarating experience that life can be. When we are in our minds we also become numbed in our ability to find compassion for those in need. For some the mind can become a prison that they have unknowingly become trapped in and that we have to learn to escape from if we want to re-find our deeper humanity. The mind does not want to feel, and it fears losing control in any way, therefore it fears the influence of emotion. It does not want us to feel our own fear; therefore it gets in the way of our becoming consciously aware of, and thus constructively working with and transcending our *subconscious fear process*. Of course the opposite can happen, we can become lost in negative emotion, and that is why it is useful to have emotional release practices to allow us to find a happy middle ground where we feel emotion and are not detrimentally ruled by it.

Emotional learning and emotional intelligence are both key to our development as whole human beings, as well as our key in supporting our ability to make wise decisions in a world made up of people who make decisions based upon emotion (whether they realize it or not). If we cannot understand other's emotional processes and our own emotions, how can we make wise decisions with those we are in relationship with? In addition, how can we live in joy and happiness if we are not even feeling our own emotions in the moment? How can we be living in constant joy, love and happiness if we are in stuck in mere logic and rationality or lost in some abstract mental process or simply in the emotionally dulled space of our mind?

I suggest complete transcendence of fear is the optimal goal. At the same time doing so is necessary in order to retain the qualities of:

- non-judgmental and unconditional love
- emotional, physical and interpersonal intimacy
- wisdom
- consciousness
- compassion
- intelligence
- creativity
- discipline
- discernment
- mutual respect
- interpersonal trust
- patience
- humility
- teamwork
- a constructive focus on evolving the quality of our life decision-making strategies

If we focus on developing these values and basing our decisions on these values we can achieve anything. Fear is our dysfunctional and unworkable *attempt to solve the pain of the past* by controlling the negative future(s) that we are imagining *could* happen. If we follow this reactive fear process we are not living in the now. Therefore we are not optimally empowered.

This process of attempting to escape our fear and pain is the source of *all addiction*; the addictive substance itself is our method of relieving the pain and distracting ourselves from what we do not want to deal with in life. Ultimately we cannot escape our fears and their associated pain and we waste much time and energy trying, and we delude ourselves in the process. If we try to fight our fears directly we are simply fighting our own negative energy and our own imaginations and painful memories.

We also try to suppress our feelings of shame, guilt and self-judgment, which are just expressions of underlying fears of not meeting our own or other's expectations. As long as we suppress these feelings they will, along with the pain associated with them, continue to plague and debilitate our lives and relationships, and disempower us fundamentally. It is necessary that we be willing to directly feel our most painful feelings in order to constructively work with them, and that we have effective tools to work with our emotions once they have been fully surfaced. There is an old saying I heard years ago which applies here, "if you cannot feel it you cannot heal it".

If rather than suppressing our pain we instead *discharge the pain* we have stored from the past then there is no more negative energy or painful emotional fuel left to "fund" the process of our fearful imaginings. If we apply an emotional release process to *consciously manage* our emotional systems on a day-to-day basis, and release our pain regularly, then we do not accumulate or store more emotional pain. Thus we will not tend to create more fear and pain and we become more able to focus in the now. The processes of releasing fear energy described in this book are designed to discharge the old pain we have acquired earlier in our lives and to give the reader methods of continually discharging any newly accumulated fear energy and pain as we move through our lives. The reason we hold onto our pain is because we *fear releasing it*. We fear releasing our pain because we fear that if we forget our pain that we may then make the same choices from the past (which we often see as mistakes or as our fault) that created it in the first place. This is erroneous decision-making and is often the result of self-judgment. We do not need to hold onto the pain of the past to help us remember the past or to learn the lessons of our past. When we release our fears then the pain we have been holding onto from past experiences tends to go with them immediately. The fear process and the pain process are in effect two sides of the same coin.

What is required to solve the problem and process of fear is to *close the gap* between our old unhealed pains and imagined projected future pain completely. When we do this we fully understand within ourselves at every level of our mind and emotional system that it is only ourselves that is generating the situation and feelings of fear. As soon as we do so the fear goes away.

Many of us want to hold onto our *old pain* because we feel that remembering old pain will remind us not to allow ourselves to be hurt in the future, or that others cannot be trusted, or even that we cannot trust ourselves and our decisions. Fear motivates us to erroneously assume that holding onto and remaining in a state of "old pain" will save us from a future situation of "new pain". This is also why we choose not to forgive ourselves and others, in that we fear that it is not emotionally "safe" to forgive, because we fear we may be hurt again if we do. This kind of thinking is completely untrue. In addition, holding onto old pain tends to keep us fixated on the past, rather than simply learning lessons from the past, and then moving on from the past. It is often only through *complete forgiveness*, either of self or others (or both) that we can become willing to release the past and become more focused on and effective in the present. It may also be that by first being willing to release our pain and fears that we can become willing to forgive. Therefore we often get stuck in our pain and the fear of it reoccurring in the future and become unable to effectively create love and joy in our present and in our future. This detrimental emotional cycle can be broken forever.

An example of this situation would be if someone got their heart broken in a relationship and then became afraid of emotional intimacy in future relationships, because they had not yet released the pain of the past. In their fear of being hurt in future relationships they would tend to avoid creating new love relationships and thereby finding joy and happiness. Another common example would be the remembrance of past failures at work leading to a fear of failing in the future, which tends to create a lack of confidence, unwillingness to risk, feelings of low self-esteem or a tendency toward unrealistic and maladaptive perfectionism in all of our decisions and actions.

Our Two Core Fears:

In reality all human beings have only two main fears, the first is the fear of death and it's assumed associated pain or discomfort. "Death" can take many forms, including the perceived death of relationships, the death of a career or the death of a cherished belief, value, dream or goal. Of course death can also include the physical death of ourselves or someone or something we love. I have spoken with several people who say they have no fear of death. Yet when asked they then say that they *do feel* great fear of dying and leaving their children without a parent, or having someone they love dearly die, or they fear dying without accomplishing a cherished goal or dream, or the actual process of dying, or they fear the pain they may feel just before death. Of course these are all fears of death or that are directly associated with death. So yes they do fear death, just certain aspects of death, types or sorts of death or things they directly or indirectly relate to or associate with death.

The second core fear is the fear of abandonment and its associated pain or discomfort. Abandonment can also take many forms, such as rejection by others, being judged by others, loss of relationships, losing a job, losing social status of any kind, or the self-abandonment we feel when we judge ourselves. We also intensely fear shaming ourselves or potentially creating situations where we believe we *would feel guilty*, since both of these situations are a form of self-abandonment via self-judgment. We fear any sense of separation from those we love, or those we feel we are in need of, and we fear the associated feelings of reduced safety, power and security that the separation brings with it. Of course we feel intensely abandoned when those we love die. So death and abandonment are tightly connected states at all levels, whether socially, mentally, physically, emotionally or spiritually. Many people even fear being abandoned by God or by their spiritual communities.

If we find the root of fear that is the first domino that leads to the down-line negative emotional state we want to resolve then we can release the fear and relieve the emotional state that we are feeling. It is just that simple and direct a process. It is *not always easy* to find the core fear however, because many of us deny and suppress our awareness of our fears, sometimes so much so that we become unaware that we are even feeling them. In addition we may be so lost and distracted in other negative emotions such as anger, guilt, shame or depression that we feel disempowered to focus on our fears and thus to effectively address and release them. The immobilizing and distracting effect of our *peripheral negative emotions* can render us unable to even understand the true nature our more deeply held core fears. In order to resolve our fears we must first accept that we can and do feel them. Then we must choose to become aware of them, identify them, and then choose to willfully and directly resolve them.

Men and women tend to handle fear differently and both have their own non-optimal methods of trying to handle it. Men in particular have often been conditioned to deny and suppress fear as if it is a sign of weakness or of not being masculine or manly. Some men have been taught that it is not socially acceptable for them to feel or express fear. Many men may literally feel socially and physically *unsafe* if they feel or show fear, or may hate their feelings of fear in that they feel vulnerable and powerless in regard to their own emotional process. This makes it very difficult for men to experience emotional vulnerability and thus to be open to emotional intimacy. This often subconscious *fear of fear* is a key reason that men do not work more with therapists or participate in couples counseling in order to resolve their emotional issues or relationship issues. This situation creates difficulties in male/female relationships when women want to relate to men emotionally and bring emotional intimacy and vulnerability into the realm of sexuality. This conflicted situation and emotional conditioning is a result of traditional societal expectations which no longer serve a purpose and which are not truly in the best interest of society or of individual men or male/female relationships. This situation also makes it difficult for men and women to consistently communicate on emotional issues in a safe and intimate way and thus resolve even basic relationship issues.

This tendency to suppress fear can make it very difficult for soldiers (both men and women) who have become traumatized and suffered from post-traumatic stress syndrome (PTSD) to constructively work with their suppressed fears and traumas. They may have been taught that they are not supposed to feel the fear and trauma that they do actually feel, and that doing so equates to failure, weakness, disloyalty and creating a state of potential vulnerability for their military comrades. They are taught that it is a sign of failure or weakness to be in a fear state, when it is in reality a very normal sign of their humanity. If we can accept that we have fear we can release it and not be affected by it, even in war. If we deny it, it can bring dysfunction at a critical moment.

Society in general is currently poorly equipped, educated or motivated to adequately facilitate, support or honor these men and women who have participated in war through their healing process. This lack of understanding on the part of the political system, and the military and the civilian population is leading to a less than adequate process of assimilation of honorably discharged veterans into civilian life. Full societal support *for the entire lifecycle* of military personnel's recovery from the effects of PTSD is necessary and is owed to those who have served their country. I am not personally an advocate of war since I do not see it as a viable solution for any of society's problems or the world's problems. I do feel that the world and the problems it faces have become far too complex and interdependent for war to be truly useful and this will only become more true as time goes by. Still I do feel that all of the problems that war itself creates must be resolved.

Fear in males in general creates a block within their emotional systems which keeps them from acknowledging and then consciously experiencing their fear in order to release it in an empowered and healthy way, and thereby permanently transcending it. Processing fear through conscious acknowledgment of it is a far better way to address fear than simply trying to suppress it, deny it, or control it. It is certainly true that courage can *temporarily* conquer fear, and it is a respectable method of addressing fear in the short term. Courage is necessary in life in order to face the trials that life presents us with and to get through life. Courage must be developed as we mature; still by itself courage is not a complete antidote to fear, acquired trauma or unresolved pain.

Suppressing fear is not healthy or functional. Suppressed fear can show itself in physical illness as well as stress reactions, anger, aggression and violence; these reactions are not healthy ways to address fear. We have seen far too many children acting out violently across America and the rest of the world. I perceive that this is simply a sign of unresolved fear and emotional stress. Once fear has been processed out of our systems we can live life in freedom, and with a sense of inner peace and tranquility. Until we resolve our fears we cannot create any state of lasting inner peace, nor can we completely love and accept ourselves or anyone else consistently. This is because our fears will continue to drive us into negative emotional states and decisions, which will in turn *drive out* our loving natures, and interrupt our intentions to love and be loved. This cyclic process need not be our fate nor that of our children.

We No Longer Know Who We Are:
In today's world many people feel lost and move through life without a clear sense of identity, purpose or understanding of who they are, where they are going, or why. The social and personal roles of the past that we have previously used to define ourselves and our feeling of life purpose no longer work. We used to use these roles to make our life decisions, now they are no longer clearly defined or understood and so our decisions are no longer clear, simple or functional. Roles of mother, father, man, woman, wife and husband have all changed dramatically in the recent past and are still changing right now. The power dynamics between men and women and parents and children are all dramatically shifting. New technologies are empowering everyone in unforeseen ways and this will only continue.

This shift in understanding of who we are, who we can be, what we can do and what affects how and why we should see ourselves as we do is rapid and unpredictable. In part this change is being driven by a rapid influx of new information which is being made available to us from many sources such as the internet, television, social media, books and rapidly changing social and work experiences. This situation is causing a sort of social emotional trauma and identity crisis and dislocation that is intensely fear producing for many people. It is also resulting in a divorce rate of about fifty percent in America and a massive problem in the emotional development of the children of these broken families. The stresses that children today feel as they grow up are often unbearable, and many have no source of adequate guidance or understandings of how to make wise decisions that will bring good results from moment-to-moment. Even families that manage to hang together in spite of this situation are still tremendously stressed by the rapid change and many unknowns the world is experiencing.

This social "change stress" and its massive effect on individuals and society need to be managed consciously rather than fearfully and unconsciously. Currently there are no really large scale efforts being created to deal with it, and this needs to change quickly. The true nature of the problem is not well understood, and is not being talked about at an adequate level of sophistication or comprehensiveness in mainstream media. However there *is much being done to feed the fires of fear* and to push average people into greater degrees of fear and stress. You can see this if you turn on the television or radio and listen to the news for five minutes.

When we talk of stress management we are in reality speaking of *fear reaction management*. Releasing stress is actually releasing fear and with it the distortion of our consciousness, decision-making and behavior that it brings. Therefore if we want to manage our reactions to rapid change in the world, and the lack of clear roles and rules, and our reactions to all of the conflict in the world, we must first identify what we fear about it all and then release what we fear. Then we will no longer have any stress and we will be in an optimal state to make wise decisions for ourselves and those we love. If for example we fear our not understanding what is happening around us and our inability to control our lives, then this is the fear we must release. Fearing not understanding what is happening will not help us to better understand anything.

There are many stresses produced in our relationships due to what we perceive to be our *expected roles,* which are currently changing rapidly or which are not clearly defined at all. There are also stresses produced when our roles are not really attainable, as when someone *expects us* to do more than we can really possibly do and we stress (translates to fear) about this situation. It is especially true that children stress when they do not have clear understandings about life, roles, rules, boundaries and what is going on around them, and they feel powerless to do anything about it. For our children, who are now growing up in a very "grey", complex, undefined, and disorienting world, it is a very stressful time. This is a time in which they can be "unfriended" on Facebook, or have their carefully constructed *cyber identities* destroyed in the social media world in an instant. Thus they can feel abandoned by the whole world, all by remote control, often without understanding how or why it all happened. Teaching them methods of *proactively* releasing their fears of rejection, criticism, being judged by others and fears of abandonment is a powerful way of helping them face this confusing and increasingly complex world situation. Teaching our children how to release their fears and thus *constructively managing* their emotional process, *before* they are faced with the need to actually do so in the real world (or the cyber world) can be an incredible gift.

It is true that the current situation of undefined or not clearly defined social and interpersonal roles, expectations and rules is stressful. It is also true that the world is changing at an incredible rate. Yet all of this, in many ways, is a positive occurrence. The roles and rules of the past are antiquated and no longer fit our increasingly complex and technologized world. It is also true that we do need many of the technologies that we are developing if we are to feed a population of nine billion people by 2050 and solve a multitude of other problems we face globally. So in effect the changes are necessary, very messy and basically good. Still technology is a double edge sword. In this process of *world re-construction* we need to develop new ways of relating to each other, of interacting socially and of being in relationship. This will take time as all learning does and will likely continue to be stressful. It will be helpful if we as individuals learn to proactively and consciously adopt stress management strategies so that we do not become emotional casualties of the global change process. The world will continue to change, faster and faster, whether we are ready for it or not. We can make the best of it, and even learn to like it, if we are willing to let go of and manage our fear of it. We can learn to creatively and joyously surf the waves of global change or be swamped by them.

As we move through our lives and develop and evolve as people it is necessary that we learn to be the best partners in our relationships that we can be. This is important not only for our own happiness, but also for the happiness of those we love and those who depend upon us. If we do learn *functional ways* to manage our emotions and our fears we can become consciously loving caring partners. If we do not we may resort to reacting to relationship stresses with feelings of fear, anger, guilt, shame, judgmentalness, aggression or other negative emotional dynamics as a *maladaptive way* of handling the stresses of life change that we all must face. I hope that you choose to find peace and love in all of your relationships.

Chapter 2: The Desire To Be In Control of Our Lives is an Addiction:

The following is a description of the detrimental side of fear driven negative emotions. It is not meant to represent a reflection of all that human beings currently are, nor is it all that we have the potential to become. This is a description of a cycle and a process that happens in all of our lives every day and that can be overcome if we choose to do so. We all have the capability to love unconditionally, to forgive and to achieve inner peace. We also have the potential to live in peace with everyone around us, *if that is our highest priority.* Fear is however often, and unknowingly, the *highest priority* in many people's lives. In the following pages we will discuss descriptions of the Cycle of "Fear Driven" Belief Creation, the Control Cycle and the Judgment Cycle. These cycle descriptions and discussions are meant to facilitate the ultimate transcendence of all of these cycles, detrimental tendencies and the results they create in our lives and in the world.

When we feel fear we immediately want to feel safe from what we fear, even if our fear does not consciously register in our mind. When we feel fear our body reacts and we "tense up" to some degree in some part of our body, even if we do not consciously realize we have done so. When we feel fear and we want to feel safe we then want to feel in control, (both men and women function this same way though they often use different methods to create their "feelings of safety" and assert control). Men can be far more physically aggressive in their attempts to control their environments and relationships than women and this is sometimes seen in a tendency to be physically violent. All motivations by both men and women to try to be dominant or to dominate in personal relationships and various social and business environments are examples of this same detrimental control tendency. Both men and women try to gain power of various kinds in order to affect control over the world around them, and over others, and over themselves, and even over their own mental and emotional processes, and their own bodies.

This process of trying to be in control has become an actual addiction to much of humanity, though it is not currently understood to be so. I am defining addiction here as any detrimental behavior, decision-making process or emotional state that we cannot consciously and consistently *"say no to".* Our controlling tendencies are for most people something they cannot say no to, as they are driven to function this way by subconscious fear. Judgmentalness itself is also an addiction, in that for most people, it has become a generally *involuntary, dysfunctional and maladaptive reaction* to trying to deal with and control life's problems and disappointments. Both control and judgmentalness are driven by the addictive emotion of fear. Acknowledging that the emotional reaction of *fear itself is an addiction,* that can be broken and transcended, and understanding its profound and detrimental influence in our lives, is the first step to disengaging from its influence forever. The addiction to fear creates and drives the addiction to control and to using judgmentalness as a method of enacting control. Letting go of these addictions is no different than letting go any other addiction, whether it be to drugs, alcohol or food. Just like any addiction we must first be willing to admit that we have a problem (i.e. that we are indeed afraid and that our fear is causing us problems in our life) in order to gain the courage and willful intentionality to then face our fears and work with our fears.

See the diagram below depicting the complete Cycle of "Fear Driven" Belief Creation. See that it is a self-reinforcing cycle, meaning that as we fear and as our fears create more of our perceived reality, the more we tend to fear, and the more we tend to believe in our fears and in what we fear. We also tend to erroneously believe more in fear and fear based decision strategies as a solution to life problems even though they do not work:

The Cycle of "Fear Driven" Belief Creation

Feeling or perceiving ourselves to be unsafe triggers and/or creates the feeling of fear, which then creates the desire for safety or feeling safer. Then we assume we need to affect the state of control in order to be safe or *safer*.

Below is a diagram which describes the Control Addiction Cycle which fear creates, fuels and holds in place.

As stated earlier, attaining complete control over anything in our lives is a myth that cannot be achieved, although many strive after it endlessly, and many of us *want to believe in it* in order to feel safe and powerful. We can optimize our personal power and influence, however functioning in either a controlling or judgmental fashion (both dynamics driven by fear) is not the best way to achieve these goals. Conscious intelligent awareness of the present moment and discerning balanced decision-making, based upon factual, accurate and complete information is a far better method. Fear does not support this process and actually works in direct opposition to it.

In order to affect the desired and imaginary state of "control" our species has developed something I will call the Judgment Cycle, which has been conditioned into most of the human species. The Judgment Cycle says that:

"I am to judge everything that I think, do, say, feel, decide, choose or want according to some combination of societal expectations, standards, traditions, rules, values, family expectations or my own expectations. Then if I do not meet those expectations or work within those rules I am supposed to punish myself in some way in order to control myself, until I do meet the expectations. "

The punishments we then choose to apply to ourselves can range anywhere from feeling guilt or shame or to getting angry at ourselves, or to hating ourselves or sabotaging ourselves in our careers or withholding from ourselves that which would otherwise bring us happiness. We also use our expectations as our rational to judge and punish others constantly in order to try to control them. Although we do influence others, we are never successful in *completely controlling* anyone. The worst examples of this process in action are in abusive relationships and in cases of child abuse. Still the same process is applied in even almost every relationship to some degree.

According to this belief system if we just judge and punish ourselves often enough and harshly enough, by whatever means, we will somehow and someday become "good people" or gain acceptance from self or others. Of course this process does not work, "someday" never comes by this process. What we are all seeking of course is the "silver bullet", meaning a strategy of total *social and interpersonal unabandonability*. One common strategy that many people have developed to try to become unabandonable is to try to be "perfect" in all areas of their lives, so that no one can judge them and then punish them by rejecting them. This strategy only creates intense stress since trying to be perfect is a process of trying to *completely control oneself*, which cannot be done, so these people are constantly stress as they constantly fail to control themselves. No strategy of unabandonability can ever truly exist, however we can release all of our fears of abandonment. We *can* become more loving people by understanding ourselves, loving ourselves and forgiving ourselves, we *cannot* achieve loving relationships by controlling, distrusting, punishing or hating ourselves.

The Judgment Cycle is a process of conditioned *self-distrust* in that we learn to fear our own self-judgment and self-punishment for any perceived wrong doing. It is also a cycle of distrusting, controlling, judging and punishing that we apply to others just as often. We also distrust and fear others judging and punishing us. How dysfunctional, unloving, disharmonious and internally conflicted a social and interpersonal situation and system is this? How can one esteem to achieve and live a life of inner peace and harmony with such a process running in their system? How disruptive to our day to day thinking and decision-making is this process of constant self-checking and socially trained and enforced self-abuse? How can society esteem to function peacefully with this fundamental dynamic running in its citizenry? How profoundly does the Judgmental Cycle detrimentally affect and distort the foundational processes of democracy and the quality of democratic institutions? How profoundly does it affect the function of our educational institutions?

Attaining complete self-trust and with it inner peace requires one to release all fear of one's self-judgment and self-punishment, *fear of making mistakes*, and to forgive oneself for past choices that did not work out well. Without release from the fear driven Judgment Cycle we remain in ongoing inner conflict and in ongoing conflict with others, whether we realize it or not. We also remain stuck in the past as we continue to ruminate over our past misdeeds, holding on endlessly to guilt and shame or holding onto anger or hatred for other's misdeeds. It is simple fear that drives this process of judgmentalness in all of its forms. We must understand that fear is such a primal and subconscious process that it neither loves nor does it have the capacity to forgive, we must rise above our fears and into a higher state of consciousness and understanding in order to love and to forgive ourselves and each other.

Many of us have been taught to manage our lives, relationships and day-to-day decisions via a comprehensive *framework of expectations* of self and others that we each consciously or subconsciously hold. This framework of expectations represents our subconscious *system of attempted control of our lives*. These expectations stem from our own set of recorded beliefs or life rules of what is true, fair, right, just or equitable, or they may just be based upon our personal desires and what we "want to be or happen" in our lives. We then tend to judge and punish and try to control ourselves and others via these referenced beliefs and projected expectations that stem from them. Our personal control strategies or always trying to be perfect, always trying to be "right" or always trying to be in control of others or ourselves are based upon this underlying system of beliefs and expectations.

If we have expectations that are not met we tend to become disappointed, frustrated, angry, judgmental, confused, sad, or even hateful. Sometimes we feel resentful and betrayed when we have cherished expectations that are not met and feel that life is unfair; this is especially true in relationships. We can be very self-righteous in regard to our expectations, without first questioning our expectations validity. A key understanding is that the reason that we have developed the whole process of expectation is that it is **only** a *system of control and fear management*. We inherently fear the unknown and unknowable future with all of its uncertainty. We assume that if we project our beliefs and their associated expectations onto ourselves, others and the world that our expectations will then give us some power and control over the future and thus keep us safe or safer. We assume that our expectations will give us some degree of increased *certainty*, and thus some influence over what we fear, and control over the attainment of what we want. These assumptions are of course false and are proven false daily, although we tend to repeatedly ignore this proof because our fears tell us to. We do this because we would much prefer to belief that we have a useful security blanket (our beliefs and expectations) that we can hold onto for safety in the face of what we fear. Expectations have no more real power than that although they constantly effect our decisions and thoughts and thus can detrimentally affect our capacity to manifest what we want if we hold negative expectations about life or relationships. In comparison, conscious awareness, wisdom, discernment and understanding of what is going on right now is truly empowering.

Unfortunately, believe it or not, many of us would actually prefer that our *worst expectations* be validated, thus giving us a sort of feeling of security, control, empowerment and the feeling that we really do understand how the world works. Even if these *mis-understandings* mean that we will end up being unhappy, unfulfilled and not get what we truly want from life, we would rather be *right*. We would subconsciously choose this negative result over having a *completely unexpected* positive result that did not support our beliefs and expectations and which would then create a feeling of deep insecurity because it would mean that we were *wrong*. This is why many of us avoid opportunities for happiness and actually sabotage ourselves. We do this by fearfully and subconsciously projecting probabilities of failure when we contemplate achieving our goals and unhappy results when we think about our relationships or careers.

Some people can be severely critical, dominating, intimidating and authoritarian in their application of their expectations towards others. Expectations often become their excuse and their "decision-making map" for threatening and punishing others, or reason for other controlling behaviors of various kinds in their relationships. This process can be seen in its most extreme form in situations of abuse, control seeking and also in what is perceived as "valid application of authority". The only difference between these three situations is that valid authority is sanctioned by some aspect of society, or by some group or organization, including family and is often assumed to be "right or unquestionable". This dominating behavior and process is often driven by an "ends justifying the means" approach to life. All forms of domination, intimidation and control seeking are generally driven by some degree of fear, rather than consciousness and wise discernment or true necessity, though the fear is often subconscious and suppressed. This is even the case in overtly dominating or over controlling parenting. Meaning there is always an optimal balance of power in any relationship that is best for all participants, including that of parents and children. Children need a certain degree of autonomy and freedom in order to develop as well as clear boundaries, rules and guidance. When parents become aware of their fears and release them they are empowered to become more loving parents and children are empowered to creatively and freely experience life and to live in their own power.

As stated earlier many negative emotional interpersonal dynamics and judgmental tendencies stem from fear of our expectations *not being met*. It is useful to realize that our expectations are often tightly tied to our desires, though we may not realize this important connection. Our conscious goals are often tied directly to our desire to maintain our safety and security. Our goals are also tied to our perceived ability to use feelings of pleasure to offset our experiences of pain and discomfort we feel in our lives. If we suddenly felt we could not control our ability to create pleasure or comfort in our lives we would tend to become afraid. We would not feel "in control". We tend to look at the comfort and pleasure we have become accustomed to, such as emotional stability in marriage, as a form of security that we can be terrified of losing. The same is true of our creature comforts, such as a warm comfortable house, a dependable car, a smart phone, the internet and cable television. Therefore I would suggest realizing that for every expectation we have, we also have an often subconscious fear of it not being met. If this is true, how many new potential fears are we creating as we create more and more desires and associated expectations in our lives?

It is our desire to control our lives and our reality, as well as our attempts to force reality to meet our expectations that often create the dynamics of negative emotions and relationship conflict. Many people fear giving up their expectations because of the *false sense of security, certainty and control* that having expectations gives them. This is because they believe that if they have expectations of others that they can then righteously judge and punish others into doing as they expect them to. They may also believe that if they have expectations of themselves that they can (and should) emotionally punish themselves into meeting their own expectations. Many of us punish ourselves constantly with feelings of shame and guilt, or through feelings of anger at self or self-hatred. We have actually been taught that this is appropriate and necessary behavior. Holding expectations and applying them to ourselves or our relationships usually only leads to conflict, confusion, misunderstanding and disappointment. I therefore suggest that releasing all expectations of self and others is the road to inner peace and peace in all of our relationships. It is useful to realize that such a significant change in consciousness itself can produce fear.

An expectation is nothing more than *a projection onto reality associated with our desires, beliefs or assumptions*. An expectation is a simply a disappointment or a conflict waiting to happen. Our expectations are in reality neither right nor wrong, neither good or bad, neither true nor false, they are only our *projections of our imaginations*. Yet we often tend to attempt to imbue our own expectations with a sense of truth, fact, necessity and validity and back them with our willfulness and willingness to punish ourselves or others if they are not met. Many of us assume we would become powerless in life if we did not follow this dysfunctional process. When we do however follow it we may then feel justified in rationalizing any sort of negative behavior on our part in order to *get our way* when our expectations are not met. We often dismiss *other's expectations* as wrong, unrighteous, unfounded and invalid. Holding onto our own expectations and the resentment we feel when they are not met blinds us to others emotional states and needs and is a key support mechanism to the mindset of *victimhood*. The process of expectations also support misinterpretations of betrayal in relationships and a general belief in the "unfairness of life".

What I am implying is that our *framework of expectations* tends to directly support and keep in place our overall *framework or system of fears*. There is at least a one to one correlation between these two systems. These two systems are mutually reinforcing, meaning that your fears motivate you to expect, and your expectations trigger and reinforce your fears. It is truly a vicious cycle. Ultimately there is no expectation that we can hold that will truly optimally serve us, or those we love. Since expectations are projections onto present moment reality they take us out of the present moment and the now, and into what we want to happen in the future or what we fear happening in the future. Thus we actually miss what is occurring in the moment, to our detriment, and we become unable to affect what is happening in the now accurately and precisely.

Our expectations actually tend to delude us with our own projected mis-information and thereby detrimentally affect the quality of our decision-making without our realizing it. If you give up projected expectations forever and completely, you can begin to simply see what is presently in front of you, and make decisions based upon that more accurate, timely, complete and factual information, rather than wasting time looking at the illusion of your own projections. Giving up expectations does not imply giving up goals or goal seeking, or conscious intentions for future accomplishments or giving up being powerfully willful in our approach to life. It only means that we focus on doing what we can to accomplish these things *in the now*, by affecting that which is truly happening in the now. This is truly our most empowered stance in regard to accomplishing our goals.

It is crucial to understand that whenever we judge anyone for anything, (including ourselves), that there is a fear of *something or someone* within us that is driving the judgment. For example if we judge someone for being a hateful person it is because in some part of ourselves we fear their hateful tendencies or their capacity to harm us or someone we care about. (Even if our fear does not register in our conscious mind). We may also fear our own capacity to hate them in the same way that they hate us. If we judge someone for their religious beliefs or other beliefs it is because in some part of us their beliefs threaten us in some way, although we may not consciously understand exactly what that threat is. For us to transcend our judgmentalness and thus the fear that drives it we must dig down within our emotional selves to find the specific fear that we are feeling. When we do determine the core fear and release it then the judgment that we have been holding toward the other person disappears immediately. Then we will be able to see the other person without judgment and have the potential to find it within ourselves to love and forgive them. We cannot love anyone we are in judgment of (i.e. in fear of), not even ourselves. In order for love to exist within us, our judgments, and by association our fear, must first go.

Oddly enough many of us are so used to judging ourselves and others we often do not even realize we are doing it. It is often in the process of perceiving ourselves or evaluating ourselves that we unknowingly get caught up in judging ourselves. It is in our process of self-perception that we subconsciously also project our fearful imaginings onto ourselves, and along with these projections we add our process of self-judgmentalness. We tend to judge our thoughts, our emotions, our behaviors and our own decisions endlessly. This then leads to our trying to control ourselves through self-punishments of various kinds and negative emotions towards ourselves of anger, shame, guilt or even self-hatred.

Judgmentalness in general has become a transparent part of our decision-making and thought process in regard to how we interact with others and how we attempt to force our opinions and will upon ourselves and others, while rationalizing how and why we are "right to do so". If we wish to cease judging ourselves and others it is essential that we raise this usually subconscious process to a level of consciousness at which we can then intervene and change our way of thinking, feeling, reacting and deciding. Otherwise we will remain "on automatic", and our unconscious and often fear driven egos will have their way endlessly, without our realizing it is happening. There is often resistance within us to bringing these parts of ourselves to full consciousness.

The Judgment Cycle has been societally and culturally implemented around the world in judicial systems, in prison systems and even in the world's educational systems. Its existence tends to create fear and mistrust in those who participate in all aspects of these systems and thus conflict and dysfunction. Our fear driven processes of judgmental blaming and "wrong making" have even made their way into our systems of government, governmental values and governmental legislative decision-making. If you question this statement simply listen to the news for a few minutes and you can see the process of ongoing mutual accusation, vilification and disparagement between political parties in any country. This has become the default method of trying to achieve goals in government for many politicians. Of course the Judgment Cycle is also the main driver for military action.

Whenever something appears to go wrong in our lives many of us assume there must always be someone to blame and we tend to assume that this process of blaming, shaming and punishing is somehow constructive, effective, positive and results oriented. We assume that blaming and punishing will achieve the results that need to be achieved in life and that people deserve this type of treatment. In this process someone always has to be right and someone always has to be wrong, this is not a recipe for compromise, negotiation or peace or teamwork. This is often referred to as "justice" and we erroneously assume that it leads to problems being solved. Often it does just the opposite.

Blaming is seen as an *empowering process* that we are afraid to let go of, and that tends to make us feel *safer* when we do it, even though it does not truly make us safer at all. Blaming actually helps us hide from self-accountability for our own emotional process, feeling and dealing with our pain, the part we played in the problems we are upset about, management of our personal power, and being accountable for the results of our life choices. The basic assumptions we hold about blaming are totally erroneous and merely tend to dig us deeper into our problems as individuals, families, social groups, religions and nations. The dynamics of blame and judgmentalness also tend to breed conflict, hatred, resentment and revenge seeking rather than a focus on true problem resolution and solving. If we instead choose to become *totally self-accountable* for both the conscious management of our emotions and the results of our life choices, and stop blaming and judging others, then we become truly empowered. We also become capable of forgiving ourselves and others. We cannot achieve inner peace until we cease to blame others for how we ourselves are *choosing to feel, no one can ever make us feel any specific way.* It is only through becoming one hundred percent self-accountable for managing our own emotional process that we can achieve a maintainable state of inner peace. This means becoming willing to give up all negative emotional states. Therefore I would ask you the reader the following question. Is living in a state of inner peace worth intentionally giving up the process of blaming and your own anger, jealousy, fear, hatred, sadness and all other negative emotional states?

The whole maladaptive developmental social system of judgmentalness has all occurred mainly because human beings simply have not known and been comprehensively taught any better way in the past to handle aberrant behavior, conflict resolution, interpersonal negotiation, misunderstandings and disagreement. We simply have not understood ourselves in the past whether socially, psychologically, emotionally or spiritually as well as we have the potential to today. In essence we have not realized how to live life as individuals, groups or as a species from the vantage point of unconditional love and compassion for self and others, and with the willingness to constantly forgive ourselves and each other.

The Judgment Cycle does not work in any venue, as for example anyone can see that people do not generally come out of prisons as more loving, caring, gentle and better societally adjusted individuals than when they went in. Certainly prison does not work to solve the problems of the mentally ill, who are being incarcerated in enormous numbers in the prison system today. The same is true in regard to the dysfunctionality of applying the Judgment Cycle to the emotional conflicts we find within ourselves. Meaning that our ongoing tendencies of self-judgment and emotional self-punishment are maladaptive and destructive rather than constructive ways of trying to manage our own emotions and behavior, even though many of us still buy into them. Self-Judgment and self-punishment only create a system of internal self-policing and self-imprisonment. Most of us do this in a very automatic and unconscious way, without even questioning whether it is wise, or deserved, or whether it will really solve the life problems it is supposed to solve in the long term.

The Judgment Cycle represents a species wide social and personal *learning disability* rather than a conscious, sovereign, intelligent and functional self-governance mechanism. The reason I refer to the cycle as a learning disability is that focusing on it and continuing to use this outdated system keeps us from understanding ourselves and others in constructive ways, as it keeps us endlessly and cyclically preoccupied judging and punishing them and ourselves. It also keeps us in reactive fear and in negative emotional states towards ourselves and others. How can we be constructively and positively learning if we are busy doing something else? We can achieve far more through conscious self-understanding, self-love, forgiveness and unconditionally loving one another. The words of Christ are completely true, ("Judge not lest ye be judged").

If we practice judging others we will also tend to internalize this process of judging and punishing ourselves, and the process will tend to cause only pain, suffering and conflict rather than achieving love, inner peace, world peace and harmony. We will also tend to teach our children to do the same thing, whether we realize it or not. The whole process is unnecessary and you can choose to break the Judgment Cycle and dismantle the fear process permanently today and forever. It is simply a conscious choice. A description of the complete negative emotional domino effect of what unresolved pain and fear leads to is listed below:

The Dynamics of Control:

1. Past pain, loss or trauma creates subconscious projections which lead to fear reactions, OR unmet expectations (subconscious projections that do not turn out to be true in reality) which trigger us to feel we are not in control of our lives, which then lead to fear.
2. When we feel the fear we then feel that we are *unsafe.*
3. This feeling of being unsafe triggers us to desire to *feel safe* or to *be safer.*
4. Which leads to the desire for *control* over ourselves or others, in order to "make ourselves safe".
5. Which leads to the desire to *acquire power* to use over ourselves or other's minds, decisions, behaviors and emotions.

6. Which leads to us to trying to control ourselves or others via judgmentalness, criticism, threats of abandonment and other forms of manipulation.
7. If these attempts do not work, then we resort to more active forms of punishment.
8. If these punishments do not work, then we feel vulnerable and powerless, and thus we resort to hatred and open violence toward self or others in order to again try to be *safe*.
9. If this process of *coercion* does not work to control ourselves or others, and we cannot "get our drug" (feeling safe and in control), we then feel even more vulnerable, powerless and angry. In this case we may turn inward against ourselves and become sad, ashamed and depressed.

This negative emotional system is unnecessary and can be consciously risen above. With conscious emotional self-management we all have the capability to transcend our negative emotional dynamics and to thereby be empowered to create consistent positive emotional states. We all have the capacity to create and hold joy and love as our highest priority in life, it is a choice that we each make every day, from moment-to-moment. It is important that we realize that we are making these choices if we want to be empowered to change them.

Chapter 3: Resolving Fear and Pain:

Poisonous animosity and resentment can build up in any relationship, sometimes over many years, and can result in repetitive arguments or even violence. In the case of marriage these emotional dynamics can also lead to divorce. These emotions are the result of the unresolved pain of the past and the constantly projected fear of potentially being hurt again in the future. They are also the result of not understanding the process of fear and how it creates the effects of the Judgment Cycle within our relationships.

There are many reflections of the two basic fears (death and abandonment) that people have created that are worth listing before we discuss the actual process of releasing fears. For example many people fear failure. Again we really only fear death and abandonment. Therefore if we fear failure it is because we subconsciously either associate our perceived failure with the possibility of some form or aspect of death or some form of potential abandonment by those we love or depend upon. If we fail we may assume that we will lose social status and value to others, and that they will no longer want to be with us or no longer want us. We may assume we will no longer have money and that others may want us only for our capability to financially support them. Therefore we will no longer be able to support them, and thus we fear we will become, in a very primal and practical way, *worthless* to them. In effect, in a financial sense, our social identity will "die". Many men have this fear since many men, even today, still see themselves as "the traditional breadwinners" of their families, though this tendency is changing rapidly as women prove themselves more than capable of earning their own money. In a world where values of competitiveness, materialism and achievement are lauded (all in the name of safety and control), failure is often looked down upon as unacceptable, therefore we fear failing.

If we have beliefs that failure is socially unacceptable or that it means that we are weak or not as good as others then we will fear being socially unacceptable and fear being seen as weak in other's eyes. This may then trigger our fears of abandonment, which can then lead to triggering our fear of "social death", even if we are not fully conscious of the process. These fears will then cause us stress and affect our decisions. It may seem totally irrational, yet to our most primal emotions, to be separated from those we love and depend upon, is basically equal to emotional death. To lose our social status or our perceived identity for example as in a divorce, is a form of emotional death. We fear this state or potential situation intensely and therefore want to avoid it. We assume that if we fear the loss of status that our fear will help us avoid it.

This is not the case; our fear simply keeps us on a treadmill of trying to avoid the loss of status, rather than taking constructive joyful action to succeed in every moment. If we release our fear we are freed to bravely and boldly take powerful action in the moment to create and manifest our reality in positive way. This is always what is needed to change our lives for the better. This is what will turn the tide of fear into the power and beauty of creation in the present. We all have this power, when we release our fears this power is no longer obscured from our consciousness.

It is useful to understand that pain can be a wonderful teacher in our lives in that it tends to point out our unwise choices, our ignorance, and the incomplete understandings we hold, as well as the need for greater balance and harmony in our lives. At the same time for many of us pain can also create another kind of learning disability when we seek to avoid it by numbing ourselves to it or by other means of hiding from it. In these situations we become unwilling to learn the lessons it offers. I would suggest that we can learn to see pain as a positive motivator in our lives and relationships and in regard to our achievement of necessary life goals. By these words I am not suggesting learning to enjoy pain or becoming masochists. I am suggesting seeing pain in a balanced way as an unavoidable aspect of life and not demonizing it and judging it and thereby *mismanaging our process of experiencing pain.*

Some of us have learned to fear and hate their pain or may have chosen to hold onto their pain endlessly, replaying it over and over in their minds, much to their detriment. Some of us feel victimized by our pain. It is always our choice how we choose to work with our pain or not to work with it at all. We can master it or become a victim of it; we can make it our best friend or our worst enemy. We can allow it to trap us in the past and limit our future or we can use it to empower us to become far greater than we could ever have been without our painful experiences. It is always our choice in every moment. In our moments of great pain this choice is rarely evident. Only later in our healing process does this understanding potentially dawn upon us.

If we wish to master our lives, our power and our potential to create our own happiness from moment-to-moment for the rest of our lives we must at some point become willing to learn how to master our process of fear and pain. Until then we will live at their mercy. We will still gain from our life experiences; we will not however be able to gain as much from them as we potentially could if we learn how to release pain and fear quickly. Nor will we gain as much learning or knowledge from our fear and pain until we are willing to see that they are potentially strengthening and educational experiences that we gain from and that we could not have become who we are without having gone through. Therefore I suggest making friends with our pain, if we do so our pain will pass more quickly and we will cease to fight it, and we can feel far more empowered to face it directly, without either fear or judgment of it. At the very least we can learn not to hate our pain. This is a type of freedom.

At this point it is useful to list a number of the basic fears that most of us have some degree of, so that you can reflect upon them in regard to the information and concepts discussed so far. Further on in the book you will be given multiple methods to work with them directly and work to release them. Many readers may assume that they have long ago outgrown their fears or have conquered them, when in reality they have actually either suppressed or denied them to the point that they no longer feel their own emotions any more. Others may have learned to focus on *other* negative emotions such as anger, judgmentalness, criticism of self or others, or even feelings of hatred, which are *just coping emotions for our underlying fears.* In this way they avoid having to face their fears and remain unaware that they are in fact even feeling fear and affected by it on an ongoing basis. In learning to live with their fears they have only learned to tolerate them, rationalize them, avoid them, disguise them and cope with them day after day.

Examples of how fears relate to other emotions are shown below:

- I fear that my spouse may abandon me and leave me for someone else who is younger or more attractive so I become angry and controlling in order to "keep them from doing so". (i.e. Anger results from unmanaged and unresolved fear).
- I fear that terrorists may attack my country so I hate them and want them killed or destroyed before they can attack me and my country. (i.e. Hatred is the result of unmanaged and unresolved fear).
- I fear that I am worthless, not good enough, a failure, and that I cannot change my life for the better. Therefore I become depressed. (i.e. Depression results from unmanaged and unresolved fear).
- I fear that I have lost a relationship that I cherish and as a result I become sad (i.e. Sadness results from unmanaged and unresolved fear)
- I fear that I have failed to meet the expectations of those I love and respect most and therefore I feel ashamed and guilty. (i.e. Shame and guilt result from unmanaged and unresolved fear).
- I fear that my spouse may want someone else more than me, therefore I become jealous. (i.e. Jealousy results from unmanaged and unresolved fear).

If our fears are resolved the resultant negative emotions become resolved. If you assume that you have conquered your fears without first checking and verifying that this is so then you will only be leaving a limitation in place in your system that will subconsciously hold you back until you do choose to face it. I suggest that being disciplined and thorough in this regard is the better route through life. Denial in regard to our fears can be very seductive and convincing though it is ultimately self-defeating.

Master Reference List of Fears Many of Us Have:

Some of the fears that most of us have *some degree of* are listed below by topic. I recommend that you read through the list and use a pencil to mark the fears that you most resonate with or can relate to. Any minor duplication of the fears listed under any category was necessary for practical support of reader's optimal usage of the reference list. Later in the book you will learn techniques for releasing these fears and you will then be able to return to this list and empowered to begin clearing the fears in a methodical and rapid manner.

Abandonment & Rejection:

The fear of / that:

- being abandoned
- feeling abandoned
- being abandoned by my spouse
- being abandoned by my girlfriend/boyfriend
- being abandoned by my children
- being abandoned by my friends or social group
- my family members might suddenly abandon me
- being abandoned by my religious community
- being abandoned by God
- I am not wanted by others
- not being wanted by my spouse
- not being wanted by my family
- not being wanted by my children
- not being wanted by my friends
- those I love and need are abandoning me
- being separated from those I love or feeling separated from them
- if I am not always focused on helping, saving or protecting others then no one will value or want me
- being rejected
- feeling rejected
- the social stigma of having been rejected or abandoned

- others will reject me if I do not conform to their expectations, beliefs, goals or values
- others will reject me if I do not submit to or resonate with their fears
- no one is ever going to understand me, and because of this no one will ever accept me
- being misunderstood
- I cannot accept myself, love myself or like myself unless others "give me permission to" or say it is okay, (i.e. I can only get my self-acceptance from others)
- no matter what I say or do I will be wrong, abandoned or will fail
- abandonment of all kinds (including criticism, punishment, being judged, emotional, sexual & social abandonment)

Addiction:
The fear of / that:

- the pain of breaking my addiction
- giving up what I am addicted to
- I have unresolvable addiction issues that will never get better
- giving up addictions of all kinds
- becoming addicted or dependent on any substance, situation or relationship
- my addiction is stronger than I am
- my fear of giving up my addiction is stronger than I am
- I do not have the will power to beat my addiction
- I will have to give up my relationships in order to break my addiction
- If I do not give up my addictions I will lose my relationships
- If I do not give up my addictions I will lose my financial stability
- If I do not give up my addictions I will lose my self-esteem, self-respect and self-worth

Betrayal:
The fear of / that:

- being betrayed by those I love, trust and depend upon most
- my spouse or lover does not really love me
- those I work for may betray me
- betraying myself
- I have betrayed myself
- my body may betray me
- my emotional or sexual impulses may overwhelm or betray me
- my government might betray me

Being Judged By Self or Others:
The fear of / that:

- being condemned by others
- self-condemnation
- being at fault or to blame in other's eyes or in my own eyes for wrong doing
- being found guilty by other's or by myself
- I have made all of the bad problems in my life happen therefore ally my problems are all my fault
- if I feel hatred for other people that it means I am a bad person
- *publically admitting* I am not perfect
- *publically admitting* I have failed or am a failure
- *publically admitting* I have broken the rules
- *publically admitting* I have made a mistake
- *admitting to myself* that I have made a mistake
- *admitting to myself* that I have failed
- not living by a set of rules that others live by
- not living by a set of rules set down by society, a social group, family, or religious group
- not doing something important with my life
- I have allowed others to ruin my life and it is my fault
- I have allow others to run or control my life and it is my fault
- if I am in pain or being punished that I must deserve it
- my situation can only get worse and that it is my fault
- admitting feelings of guilt, shame or wrongdoing
- my self-judgments and tendency to emotionally punish myself
- my self-judgments and my hatred of myself
- forgiving myself for hating myself
- forgiving myself for punishing myself
- hating myself because I will never be good enough
- forgiving others for the harm have done to me or hurt they have caused me in the past
- not being attractive enough to be acceptable to others or to be loved
- I can only achieve in life and motivate myself by self-judgment and self-punishment
- I can only achieve and motivate myself by stressing myself, judging myself and forcing myself to do what I feel I must rather than through loving myself and my work or through joyful activities

Child Abuse or Other Kinds of Relationship Abuse:
The fear of / that:

- facing my abuser and standing up to my abuser
- standing up for myself
- being abused again
- being harmed by my abuser

- being harmed by my father/mother
- being killed by my father/mother
- being assaulted by my father/mother
- being controlled by my father/mother
- being controlled by my abuser
- being powerless in regard to my abuser
- being a victim of my abuser
- being hurt by my father/mother
- being hurt by my abuser
- not being in control of my body
- others controlling me or my body
- not being in control of my emotions
- others being in control of my body, mind and my emotions
- losing control of my mind, body or emotions
- not being in control of my body, mind or emotions
- being dominated by my abuser
- being dominated by my father/mother
- being coerced or forced by my abuser
- living in terror of my abuser
- never getting past my fears of my abuser
- never completely healing from my abuse
- the social stigma of sexual assault or rape
- the social stigma of sexual abuse

Connecting With Others Vs. Independence & Sovereignty:
The fear of / that:

- I am emotionally disconnected from others
- I am becoming more emotionally distant from those I love
- I am becoming more emotionally distant from those I love and I do not know why
- those I love and need are distancing themselves from me
- I cannot truly connect with others
- I do not know how to truly connect with others
- I do not know who I am emotionally
- I do not understand myself emotionally
- I am not being truly "met" in my most intimate relationships
- being different or being seen to be different than other people
- acting in a sovereign manner in a world where everyone would like to run my life
- not submitting to what everyone else thinks is right or correct behavior
- I cannot be my true self around other people
- others will not really want me for my true self

- speaking my truth to those I love and need
- saying what I most need in my closest relationships
- saying no when it is my best interest to do so in my relationships
- setting clear boundaries in my relationships
- maintaining clear boundaries in my relationships

Control:

The fear of / that:

- I am losing control of my life
- I am losing control of my emotions and feelings
- I am losing control of my finances
- I am losing control of my mind
- I am losing control of my thoughts
- I am losing control of my relationship(s)
- not living by everyone else's rules, expectations and beliefs
- being controlled by everyone else's rules, expectations and beliefs
- if I do not control other people and their attention that it could lead to me being abandoned by them
- I can only be safe by controlling my life, life situations and relationships
- I cannot control how my spouse or lover feels about me
- I cannot control my spouse's decisions and actions in regard to me or my children
- my emotions and fears are irrational or "too extreme" or uncontrollable
- being out of control
- I never had control of my life
- no one has control of their lives and what this means
- If I do not control my life that I will die or be abandoned
- I cannot control my own thoughts, emotions, decisions or behaviors
- if I don't control others that they will control me
- my uncertainty about the future, a relationship or a situation
- lack of "perceived control" of all kinds (my relationships, my career, my financial situation, my future, my physical body, how I choose to live or to die, how others see me, etc.)
- being controlled by others
- I cannot control my life
- I cannot control my spouse
- I cannot control myself
- letting go of:
    - control
    - dominance
    - judgmentalness

    - being right
    - addiction
    - criticism
    - agendas
    - desires
    - fear
    - pain
    - anger
    - resentment
    - disappointment
    - jealousy
    - hatred
    - attachments of all kinds (i.e. to relationships, habits, goals, possessions, money, tradition, material wealth, dreams, any emotional state, beliefs, etc.)
    - *expectations* of self and others
- not having or getting what I want exactly when, where, how and why I want it
- not getting my way
- realizing that although I am not in control of my life I am co-creating it with everyone else and thus I do have power and that I am accountable for that fact

Desperation:
The fear of / that:

- I cannot keep going with my life in spite of all of the pain and suffering I have endured in my life
- I cannot do what I must do in my life in order to hold my life together and succeed
- my life just isn't working and I don't know why or how to fix it
- everyone is out to get me
- everyone is against me
- no one wants to help me
- no one understands me
- I am alone in the world
- there is nothing I can do to help myself
- things are only going to get worse and there is nothing I can do about it
- everything I do to try to fix my life just makes things worse
- I will never figure out how to solve my problems
- I am at the end of my rope
- I have no options left

- I have no power to help myself or to change my situation for the better

Decision-Making:
The fear of / that:

- making decisions
- making wrong decisions
- my own indecisiveness
- making wrong decisions and then having to live with the results of those decisions for the rest of my life
- not being able to make a decision
- I cannot trust myself not to make decisions that will hurt myself
- I cannot trust others not to make decisions that hurt me
- being confused and unable to make decisions about what I should do in my life
- I am a victim of myself and all of my past choices and decisions
- I have no other choice than to be afraid
- all of my decisions will only end up in pain and sadness
- all of my decisions are always wrong and stupid and therefore my future will never be happy
- I never make the right choices
- I always want the wrong things
- I always listen to the wrong people when I make decisions
- I will allow others to influence my decisions to my detriment
- I won't stand strong in my decisions and therefore I won't get what I want or need most in my relationships
- I don't have the will power to make strong decisions
- *not having* something I intensely want or am passionate about in my life that I can use to focus my life, and can use to select my goals and to guide my decision-making
- making powerful decisions that successfully lead me to complete self-empowerment, self-reliance, financial independence and freedom
- what I most desire may not be worth having

Expectations:
The fear of / that:

- the pressure of other's expectations on me
- not meeting my own expectations of myself
- failing to meet my own expectations or other's expectations
- my expectations may be "wrong"
- others may know better than I do and therefore their expectations are correct and mine are not

- I cannot escape other's expectations
- I will be crushed by other's expectations
- my failure to meet other's expectations will lead to punishment
- my failure to meet other's expectations will prove that I am worthless and not good enough
- even if I meet other's expectations they may not accept or reward me
- being punished for not meeting other's expectations
- being abandoned for not meeting other's expectations
- any of my physical characteristics *not meeting my own or anyone else's expectations* and this leading to my being *abandoned, criticized or not being accepted or loved* (i.e. my height, weight, hair, face, eyes, breasts, arms, legs, stomach, behind, sexual organs, teeth, or any other part of my body)
- my clothing choices not meeting other's expectations or standards
- *not* living life by other's expectations (we can fear changing to independently living life by our own free-will or set of rules, *rather than living by other's expectations*)
- I could work very hard, endure great pain, discomfort or hardship and then find out that others don't want me, accept me or reward me and I won't get what I want or what I worked for

Family Issues:
The fear of / that:

- failing to take good care of my family
- failing to be a good father/mother/son/daughter
- I must submit to my father's/mother's fears or negative emotions
- I must submit to my father's/mother's control
- I must submit to my father's/mother's abuse
- I have ruined my children by how I raised them and there is nothing I can do to change the situation for the better
- my family obligations and the guilt and shame I feel when if I do not meet them
- my children may repeat all of the same mistakes I have made and it is all my fault
- I have hurt my family and there is nothing I can do to change the situation for the better
- disgracing my family by my actions, behaviors or addictions
- being abandoned by my family
- I cannot protect my home and family
- my children are not safe
- my children are not safe at school
- I cannot control my children's activities on social media
- my children may not succeed in life

- another child could bring a gun to school and my child could be hurt or killed
- the school system is not adequately protecting my child
- my children are not safe with their friends or could be negatively influenced by their friends
- my children might start taking drugs
- my children might drive a car under the influence of drugs or alcohol
- my children might start having unprotected sex
- my child might get pregnant
- my child might get sick or die before I do
- my child may not get the education they need to survive in the coming world
- I may not be around to protect my child in the future when they most need me
- my parents might get sick or die
- losing my parents
- accepting that my mother/father *has* died
- accepting that my child *has* died
- having to go on living my life without my loved one who has died
- facing all of the problems of life alone
- I will "become" my mother/father
- I will repeat my mother's/father's mistakes
- being unable to work to provide for my family
- the world is changing too fast and in too many ways for me and my family to remain safe
- my spouse and children will not be safe in the coming world
- my way of parenting may end up harming my children
- being embarrassed or disgraced by the actions of my spouse, children or relatives
- the guilt and shame I feel about getting divorced and failing my children as a parent
- the guilt and shame I feel about getting divorced and failing in my marriage
- I cannot control my children's behavior or choices
- I cannot keep my children from making dangerous choices
- my past poor choices have hurt my family and there is nothing I can do to change this

Failure:
The fear of / that:

- failure itself
- failure to meet other's expectations or standards
- failure to meet my own expectations or standards

- failure in my marriage
- failure in my closest relationships
- failing my family
- failing to be a good wife/husband/father/mother/son/daughter
- failing in my career or to do my job
- failure to follow my own or other's rules or beliefs, or those of a religion, group or society
- failing to meet society's expectations
- failing to meet my own expectations of myself
- failing to reach my potential
- failing to keep my promises
- failing to remain honest and in integrity
- failing to help and support those I love
- failing to help those in need
- failing to gain other's respect, acceptance and approval

Fears of the Larger World Around Us:
The fear of / that:

- being fired from my job due to the economy
- being fired from my job because my boss does not like me
- the economy might fail
- terrorists attacking or of potential war
- the Ebola virus, the Bird Flu, Global Warming, pollution, Cyberattacks, unmanaged government spending, inability of government to effectively govern, unfettered governmental power, etc.
- I cannot trust the government to keep me safe
- I cannot trust the government not to spy on me
- my investments might suddenly become valueless
- I cannot understand what is happening in the world around me
- I might lose my home and security
- I will not remain financially stable in the future
- my skill sets or work knowledge will not be marketable in the future
- my spouse may leave me and that I will be alone with responsibilities I cannot handle

Feeling Trapped:
The fear of / that:

- I am *trapped* in an unhappy relationship or marriage
- I am trapped in the role of mother / father / husband / wife / caregiver / victim / rescuer
- I am trapped in my sick, unhealthy or dysfunctional body
- I am trapped in my dysfunctional emotional state

- I am trapped in dysfunctional patterns of emotion, relationship or behavior
- I am trapped in my own fear
- I am trapped in my tendency to worry
- I am trapped in confusion
- I am trapped in conflict
- I am trapped in my tendency to procrastinate
- I am trapped in my own laziness
- I am trapped in my negative emotions
- I am trapped in my negative behaviors or reactions
- I am trapped in my anger and hatred
- I am trapped in sadness, jealousy, regret, guilt or shame
- I am trapped in my own limitations
- I am trapped in poverty or lack of education
- I am trapped in other's negative emotions and intentions towards me
- I am trapped in other's negative perceptions of me or beliefs about me
- I am trapped in a dead end situation or job
- I am trapped by my own past choices
- I am trapped by my inability to change
- I am trapped by other's inability to change
- I am trapped in my old age
- I am trapped because I am not considered an adult
- I am trapped because I am not respected
- I am trapped because I have no power to free myself or change my situation
- I am trapped in the past and what happened that I cannot change
- I am trapped in my focus on the future and all of the bad things that might happen
- I am trapped in worry, anxiety, insecurity, confusion and uncertainty (a combination of states)
- I am trapped in security and safety seeking
- I am trapped in survival mode
- I am trapped in the complexity of my life and relationships
- I am trapped in the drama of my life or other's dramas
- I am trapped in my own ignorance
- I am trapped in other's ignorance
- I am trapped in other's bias or prejudice
- I am trapped in my own bias or prejudice
- I am trapped in other's selfishness
- I am trapped in other's expectations or value judgments
- I am a man trapped in a woman's body
- I am a woman trapped in a man's body
- I am a prisoner of other people's fears

Forgiveness Related Fears:
The fear of / that:

- forgiving myself
- I *should not* forgive myself for my misdeeds or prior choices or behaviors
- I won't be able to forgive myself
- I won't be able to forgive my spouse
- I won't be able to forgive my children
- I won't be able to forgive my parents
- I won't be able to forgive my abuser
- I won't be able to forgive the person who hurt or abandoned me
- I am not worthy of forgiveness
- I am unredeemable, unacceptable and unforgivable
- forgiving myself right now and forever for everything bad, negative, wrong or harmful that I have ever been or done
- I cannot do enough good works to redeem myself, therefore I will never be accepted or acceptable to others or to God
- not being worthy of being loved by God or of being in loving relationship with God
- my soul being irrevocably tainted, corrupted or stained by any past action, choice, behavior, thought or decision

Identity Related Fears:
The fear of / that:

- losing my identity, "personal space" or territory
- not being able to remain separate from others, of becoming emotionally enmeshed with others and losing my separate identity, power, space and decision-making capability
- having my identity stolen or misused
- having my reputation damaged
- being gossiped about in a damaging way
- getting caught up in social or relationship dramas and losing my sense of individual self in the process

Integrity & Honesty:
The fear of / that:

- I am not as completely honest or truthful as I feel I should be
- I cannot be totally honest with others
- I cannot be totally honest with myself
- speaking my truth
- other's lack of integrity
- others will lie to me

- others will try to use or manipulate me
- that others will see through my lies
- that others will judge me as not being in integrity

Lack & Loss Related Fears:
The fear of / that:

- "lack" of all kinds (money, love, emotional intimacy, connectedness to others, self-trust, security, certainty, sex, confidence, empowerment, self-sovereignty, etc.)
- not having enough money
- not having enough sex
- not having enough time
- not having enough food
- not having enough control
- not having enough information
- not having enough friends
- not having enough attention or recognition
- not having enough freedom
- being hungry, thirsty or without basic necessities
- of being homeless and living on the streets
- losing everything I have worked for
- not understanding what is happening in my life
- not having the resources to help those I love

Life Changes & Transformation:
The fear of / that:

- death or dying
- opening to change and transformation in all areas of my life
- having my point of view or reality changed or invalidated by someone else
- no matter how hard I work I will never be able to change myself
- major life changes of all kinds
- my life is changing in ways I cannot control and do not understand
- technology is changing too fast for me to keep up with it
- I cannot keep current with all of the learning that is required in my career field
- changing to a new career field that I have no experience in
- being forced to change to a new career field
- not being able to positively change myself, my situation, my life or my relationships
- what I will become or my life will become if I do change my self
- giving up my safety and security in order to bring positive change in my life

- I may change in some way in the future and my spouse may cease to love me
- my spouse may change in some way in the future and I may cease to love them
- I cannot change the way I feel about my work, my relationships or myself for the better
- my life will never change for the better
- the pain, stress, guilt and fear I will feel if I tell those I love that I want to fundamentally change my life
- learning something new
- learning a new language
- learning about a new technology
- the process of learning in general

Limitations and Feeling Stuck:
The fear of / that:

- I am to blame for other people's emotional states, reactions, dramas and processes
- I am bad and wrong unless I feel guilty, fearful and ashamed
- being stuck in self-punishing behaviors or relationship dynamics
- I have not fully released *all of my fears* and they will therefore continue to undermine my life
- not being able to express myself clearly, completely, honestly, openly or accurately
- being caught between the fear of moving forward and the fear of falling behind where I perceive others to be
- I won't perform well in some area of life
- I have to feel guilty and ashamed otherwise I will be seen to be egotistical and selfish
- I have nothing to give that others really want
- I will never be accepted and I will always be rejected
- I will never be able to reach other people emotionally
- no matter what I do I will always be rejected
- no matter what I do I will always remain on the "side lines of life"
- I am stuck in dysfunctional behavior patterns or relationship patterns
- I will never unlearn my detrimental behaviors or patterns
- I can only achieve my life goals in reaction to my fears rather than through self-loving motivations or for the sake of my own happiness
- I can only achieve happiness by first making myself unhappy in some way or depriving myself in some way of something that I love or want
- my own limitations of all kinds
- my fears continuing to keep me stuck forever

- being limited or constrained by anyone else or any situation
- my limited financial situation
- my lack of education
- my lack of social connections or friends
- living life without any limitations at all
- I won't be able to recover from the problems I am dealing with
- giving up being in denial
- falling back into old habits, behaviors or tendencies
- I will not live the life I was meant to live
- I am not strong enough to endure what life may throw at me
- I do not love myself enough to keep going when life is difficult
- my heart is irrevocably broken or damaged and will never be whole again
- my mind is irrevocably broken or damaged and will never be functional again
- I cannot break my addiction(s)
- I am not strong enough to face my fears
- I am *going to be afraid* if ... (I see something specifically fear producing, experience something specifically fear producing, go someplace specifically fear producing, see someone I fear, someone says something specifically fear producing, I cannot think of the right thing to say in a social situation, etc.)
- self-sabotage
- others will bring out the worst in me or that I have allowed others to do this in the past
- I will never be allowed to achieve my potential
- I will not live up to my true potential
- my pain will never go away
- I am to blame for every problem that I am facing in my life
- I must be punished in order to be redeemed, so that I can again be a good person and become acceptable to others
- I will never be happy again, no matter what I do
- I have wasted my life and it is too late for me to do anything about it

Love:
The fear of / that:

- I am unlovable and cannot do anything to make myself lovable and therefore will never be lovable
- allowing myself to be fully, completely and unconditionally loved
- I will never let anyone want or love me for who I am
- I will never learn to love or trust anyone again
- the depth of my own love
- the pain that comes with loving and being loved

- disappointing those I love or those who need me
- I do not really know how to love or receive love from others
- expressing my emotions openly
- opening my heart
- not being loved and that "I will never be loved"
- my dreams for my relationship will not come true
- harming myself or others I love through my actions or negative emotions
- love inevitably leads to pain and loss
- no one loves me
- everyone I love leaves me
- everyone I love rejects me
- all of my love relationships will end up the same way
- not being physically attractive enough to be acceptable to others or to be loved

Money Fears:
The fear of / that:

- not having enough money
- losing my money
- there is never enough money
- people are always trying to take my money from me
- I may be cheated out of money
- people only want me for my money
- my relationships may not be in emotional integrity and may only be based on financial security
- I cannot trust my spouse or my children in regard to money
- I cannot trust my friends in regard to money
- I cannot trust my own decisions in regard to money
- people with money can hurt me and have more power than I do
- people will only respect me if I have money
- being financially destitute
- I am not good at managing money
- I do not know how to make money
- I am not good at making money
- other people are better at making money than I am
- I will never have enough money
- I will always be broke or poor
- I have ruined my financial life and it is all my fault
- I am too old to make it financially
- If I had money I would only throw it away or misuse it
- If I had money my addictions would run rampant
- If I had money people would only want me for my money

- If I had a lot of money it would mean that I must have done something wrong to get it
- If I have a lot of money it means I am a selfish or greedy person
- If I have a lot of money others will try to take it from me
- If I have a lot of money I will have to give it away to others more in need than myself

Extraordinary Medical Procedures or Issues:
More and more people these days are becoming recipients of organ transplants and extraordinary medical procedures. There are a number of fears that are specific to these types of operations, as well as the recovery from the operations and the ongoing management of oneself afterward. Since it is likely that this type of operation is likely to become more prevalent in the future I am including a separate list for those readers who fall into this category.

The fear of / that:

- I may die from my transplant operation
- I may die if I choose not to get the transplant
- I may die if I do not get my transplant operation in time
- the medical system may not be able to find a proper donor for me in time
- I may not fully recover after the operation even though I have a transplant
- my transplant surgery may not go well and I may be required to depend upon machines to keep me alive for an unknown period of time
- my transplant may be partially rejected and cause other physical problems and types of illness
- I may be required to be hospitalized for a long period of time in order to recover from my transplant operation
- I may not be able to afford all of the costs of the organ transplant and the support I require afterward
- My insurance may not cover all of the medical costs and I may be left financially devastated
- I may not be able to work after I get an organ transplant
- I will be too much of a burden upon my friends and family if I get the organ transplant
- I may never have the quality of life that I had or want to have if I get an organ transplant
- I may contract an illness or infection due to the organ transplant and be worse off than I was
- I may reject the organ that is transplanted into my system

- I may not live as many years after the transplant as I want to or expect to
- I will not be the same person that I was after the organ transplant
- others may look at me differently after I get an organ transplant
- I may feel guilt or some form of emotional discomfort that someone else had to pass away in order for me to continue to live
- I may not be able to afford all of the medications after the transplant that I need to remain healthy
- I do not have control of the whole process of my health
- I do not have control of the whole process of my organ transplant
- I do not have control over my whole process of recovery
- I do not have control over my future
- I have unresolvable physical issues that will never get better

Managing Negative Emotions, Pain and Depression:
The fear of / that:

- of feeling:
    - guilty
    - ashamed
    - powerless
    - worthless
    - angry
    - hateful
    - depressed
    - jealous
    - anxious
    - resentment
    - worry
    - judgmental
    - disgusted
    - self-righteous
    - egotistical
    - better than others
    - arrogant
    - sexual
    - destructive
    - vengeful
    - dirty
- Any of these fear states which are each actually very different fear states:
    - feeling my fear
    - feeling afraid
    - feeling the feeling *of* fear

    - being afraid
    - that I *am* afraid
    - feeling scared
    - feeling in terror
    - feeling horrified
- being "hurt again" as I felt I was hurt in the past
- paralyzing depression
- feeling depressed
- getting depressed
- the effects of depression on my life and relationships
- I have no choice but to hate myself for my failings or limitations
- there is nothing I can do to solve my problems
- I may not be able to deal with the emotional pain of my own life if I choose to look at it directly
- my own negative emotional reactions
- my own pain
- my own anger
- acknowledging the pain I have caused others
- I cannot escape the pain that I feel (this statement can be useful for anyone lost in pain, it may also be useful for those who are addicted in various ways)
- I am alone in my fear, pain, shame and guilt and no one else understands how I feel
- not being appreciated
- I am a victim of my own fear
- my own internal emotional conflict
- being stuck in my own fear forever
- I am not special
- inadequacy in any area of life
- my own destructiveness
- my negative emotions
- I have unresolvable emotional issues that will never get better
- I have unresolvable mental issues that will never get better
- allowing myself to feel my own feelings
- taking responsibility for my own life
- feeling that which I am unwilling or too afraid to feel my emotions (this works well on suppressed feelings)

Not Feeling Accepted By Self or Others:
The fear of / that:

- I am not good enough
- having to explain myself to others
- being marginalized

- being seen as unimportant or as a second class citizen
- no one will know or care how I feel, how hard I work, how much I care or how much I give
- ending up old and alone
- fully realizing and accepting who and what I am
- I am being treated with prejudice or bias
- I am being treated unfairly
- others will be dishonest with me
- because I am not good enough, I am therefore undeserving of love, happiness or abundance
- not being physically attractive enough to be acceptable to others or to be loved

Phobias:
The fear of / that:

- various kinds of phobias (a more extreme and visceral sort of fear)
    - heights and falling
    - closed in spaces
    - germs and disease
    - darkness
    - insanity
    - spiders and other insects
    - snakes
    - dogs
    - men
    - relationships
    - heaven and hell
    - ghosts and the supernatural
    - I have a phobia
    - I am a hypochondriac

Physical Body Image, Aging, Illness, Appearance, Weight Management & Dying:
The fear of / that:

- death or dying
- illness of all kinds
- growing old and becoming physically or mentally dysfunctional (i.e. all aspects of the process of aging and the dysfunctions it brings including the social status changes it brings)
- growing old alone and sick and without financial support
- the stigma of old age
- the social stigma of illness
- the social stigma of physical dysfunction

- the social stigma of mental or emotional dysfunction
- the social stigma of being overweight
- those I love or depend on dying
- my negative emotions or thoughts will cause me to have a disease
- becoming physically incapable or even immobilized as I age
- gaining weight or being overweight
- losing weight or going on a diet will be too hard to do or that I cannot do it
- I cannot lose weight no matter what I do
- if I do lose weight I will not be able to meet other's expectations when I am more attractive
- no one will want me or love me if I am overweight or fat
- if I do lose weight and am more physically attractive that then I will not be able to meet other's relationship expectations
- making myself sick or ill through my choices, lifestyle or behavior
- the pain that my illness may cause me in the future
- my long term or chronic pain
- my long term or chronic illness
- the pain of dieting
- the pain of quitting smoking
- I am "broken" or cannot be fixed in some fundamental way
- going blind or losing my eyesight
- I have unresolvable physical issues that will never get better
- not being attractive enough to be acceptable to others or to be loved
- I am never going to be fully healed, whether it is mentally, physically, emotionally or spiritually

Personal Power, Usage of Personal Power, Powerlessness & How Other's Power Affects Us:

The fear of / that:

- not "having a say" and power or influence in all decisions in all areas of my relationships
- one thing going wrong in my life means that everything in my life could or is going to go wrong or is a problem
- other people's power in my life
- experiencing and expressing my feminine emotional side and power
- experiencing and expressing my masculine emotional side and power
- realizing my own power, and of openly expressing and using my power
- seeing and fully realizing my own power and of what I will do with my power when I do
- I have handed my power over to others

- taking back my power
- I am powerless in regard to others making me feel guilty
- being powerless and powerlessness
- I am powerless to change my life for the better
- being too powerful or misusing my power
- I am powerless to help myself and those I love
- I cannot trust myself in how I might use my own power
- not having enough power
- authority figures and their power over me
- seeing and accepting exactly how my own free-will choices have created my life results
- being fully grounded and living in the now and in the present moment
- not playing the world's "fear game" anymore and choosing to live a life of happiness and prosperity from now on
- not being heard
- being seen by others only in physical terms (i.e. women or men being sexually or physically objectified or being looked down upon for not being attractive enough at work, socially or in relationships)
- If I do not decide my life others will decide my life for me
- being more disciplined whether it be spiritually, emotionally, physically, sexually or at work
- acknowledging that the problems I am experiencing are of my own creation
- having no clear direction in life
- not getting what I want
- having what I want
- social competition
- relationship competition
- work or career competition
- the power of my own imagination to run away with me and to overwhelm me with fear
- I have the power of complete free-will and therefore can never truly be a victim of life or any other person
- the rug being pulled out from under my life, without warning, and that I will be left alone, and with no money or support

Relationship Fears:
The fear of / that:

- I cannot live or exist unless I am in a relationship
- I will die if I lose my relationship
- men are all bad
- women are all bad

- men are all bad and relationships have nothing to offer me but pain, disappointment or sadness
- women are all bad and relationships have nothing to offer me but pain, disappointment or sadness
- getting married and the lifelong commitment of marriage
- fully emotionally committing to a relationship
- my relationship will fail and that it will be my fault because I did not try hard enough or give enough
- my spouse or lover is not really committed to me or the relationship
- my spouse or lover does not love me exactly the same way or to the same degree that I love them
- I do not love my spouse or lover the same way or to the same degree that they love me
- I may fall out of love with my spouse or lover at some point in the future
- my spouse or lover may fall out of love with me at some point in the future
- my spouse may take everything from me in a divorce
- I cannot be happy unless all of the people in my life that I love are happy first
- being "unfriended" on Facebook or being attacked in social media
- I have to prove that I am worth loving
- I am only acceptable if others tell me I am
- revealing my true self to others
- the pain I will feel if I fail in my relationship
- the pain I will feel if I get divorced
- accepting that I am in an abusive relationship and being willing to do something about it
- I am a prisoner of other people's fears
- I cannot be what I want to be unless others allow me to
- not getting what I most want and need from my relationship
- being emotionally hurt in relationships
- being disappointed by life or relationships
- being alone
- being left behind by those I love
- those I love being hurt
- my own tendencies to emotionally react to situations or relationships
- becoming lost in my own emotions
- facing or confronting my spouse or mates anger, fear, criticism or rejection
- allowing myself to feel my own feelings
- giving up on a dream or a relationship that I realize will never happen
- taking responsibility for my own life

Safety:
The fear of / that:

- I am unsafe
- I am only safe if I am in control of my life
- I am only safe if I am in control of my relationships
- I am only safe if I am in control of my emotions
- I am only safe if I am perfect
- I am only safe if I am not vulnerable to others
- I am only safe if I am in my mind and my emotions are shut down
- I cannot protect my "territory" (relationship, career, workspace, physical, political, economic or social)
- I cannot be emotionally safe with anyone
- risking my financial security
- risking my emotional security
- risk of all kinds
- it is not safe to let go of my fears
- not being safe in life without having all of my fears to tell me when to be afraid
- if I do not continue to fear, that I will never be safe
- not being perfect
- if I am not perfect that I am not safe
- I can only be safe or accepted if I am perfect
- being attacked in the dark
- others will hold me back from achieving my dreams
- facing my fears
- admitting having negative emotions toward myself or others
- people who do not share my beliefs (including religious or political beliefs)
- people with extreme or negative beliefs
- releasing my fears (because I believe they are keeping me safe and that I will become unsafe if I release them)
- taking responsibility for my own life
- physical assault or being robbed
- if I give up all my fears I will not be able to protect myself and those I love because I believe I have to be able to fear in order to be able to be safe
- if I give up my fears that I will no longer know "when to be afraid" (as if there actually is any *good time* to be afraid or to live in fear)

Self-Expression and Creativity Fears:
The fear of / that:

- expressing myself creatively

- creating what I fear most in my life
- my dreams for my life will not come true
- wanting what I most want in life or in my relationships or in my heart
- being all that I truly am and have the capability of being
- I am not doing what I was put on this earth to do or born to do
- I will live my life only to find that I missed out on doing what I came here to do
- being disappointed by life, love, relationships, others or myself
- not being effective enough in accomplishing my life goals
- I do not deserve to have what I want or should not have what I want
- my own resistance to becoming aware of my fears
- I do not understand myself
- fully seeing, comprehending and understanding everything that I experience in life without fear
- not having a teacher, guide, guru or mentor
- fear itself
- risking living a powerful creative life
- I might give all I have to achieve my dreams and then be disappointed
- not achieving my goals
- not having truly lived

Sex & Intimacy Fears:
The fear of / that:

- intimacy and of not having intimacy
- being physically or intimately touched
- getting close to another person
- intimacy leading to vulnerability
- intimacy leading to commitment I am not ready for
- being intimate with someone who does not really love me
- not having enough sex
- not having my sexual needs met by my relationship partner / spouse
- men only want me (a woman) for sex rather than for a whole and intimate relationship
- women only want me for security (a man) rather than a whole and intimate relationship
- I am not certain who I am sexually or what my sexual orientation is
- my sexuality is tainted or corrupted due to my life and relationship experiences
- I have unresolvable sexual issues that will never get better
- sexual assault or rape
- the social stigma of sexual assault or rape
- the social stigma of sexual abuse

- being lied to in a relationship
- sexually transmitted diseases
- the guilt and shame of giving others sexually transmitted diseases
- the social stigma of sexually transmitted diseases

Social Image, Self-Worth, Social Interaction & Social Status:
The fear of / that:

- success
- competition
- public embarrassment
- embarrassing myself
- of being embarrassed by someone else
- being humiliated
- *the fear* of being humiliated
- becoming all that I can be
- realizing or accepting that I am afraid
- having others realize that I am afraid
- having others realize just how afraid I really am
- having others realize that I cannot manage my fear
- having others see me as a weakling or a coward
- not getting other's approval
- my own inadequacy
- not being seen to be equal to others
- being treated as less than others
- having my emotions invalidated by my spouse or partner
- being emotionally invalidated by others
- being mentally invalidated by others
- having my stated position in my relationship invalidated by my spouse or partner
- having my most important beliefs invalidated by those I am in relationship with or seeking approval from
- others will "see through me" and realize I am not as good as I want to be perceived to be
- being gossiped about or slandered
- being "unfriended" on Facebook or attacked in social media
- expressing or showing fear or vulnerability *publically*
- I do not matter to those I love or to the world
- I am worthless
- I am "nothing" to anyone else
- I am, as a person, unredeemably tainted or corrupted
- I am unworthy, worthless or valueless
- I will not like who I am when I fully realize who I am
- I am not a good communicator

- I must submit to everyone else's fears
- standing out publically
- showing all of my talents
- fulling realizing all of my talents and abilities
- not being physically attractive enough to be acceptable to others or to be loved
- I am only "whatever I have labeled myself or others have labeled me to be at any point in my life" ... i.e. (Stupid, fat, ugly, an idiot, not good enough, not important, a slut, useless, a divorcee, a failure, a loser, a waste, a person who will never make it, an angry person, a bitch, a bad person, a liar, broken, a fool, someone who does not matter, a coward, weak, a bad employee, a drunk, a drug addict, evil, wrong, hateful, incapable, emotionally unavailable, frigid, a geek, ...)
- being harmed by others
- public shaming
- not being understood
- being misunderstood
- being seen by others as egotistical
- being seen by others as unprepared
- not pleasing others
- if life does not make sense to me that it means I am crazy
- test taking
- job interviews
- public speaking
- asking for a raise (this is especially true for women who have been marginalized by society)
- other's fearfulness
- other's greed
- other's negativity or other's negative emotions
- others can hurt me
- the group I am a member of being embarrassed or losing status, power or safety or having its reputation damaged (including my nation)
- I am "crazy or going crazy"
- not being as smart, intelligent, educated, streetwise or experienced as other people
- not being seen and recognized by others as I want to be
- being publically discredited or damage to my reputation
- losing my personal integrity and personal sense of honor
- losing the capacity to tell right from wrong
- my own capacity to hate
- the pain I will feel if I fail at achieving my goals

Spiritual Issues:
The fear of / that:

- becoming spiritually egoless in an egotistical world
- submitting to God (however you may conceptualize God)
- I have unresolvable spiritual issues that will never get better
- my soul has lost its way from God
- I am spiritually lost and do not know how to find my way
- being misled by false spiritual leaders
- I cannot fully trust my own spiritual decisions
- I am not in true alignment with God and with my soul's intent for this lifetime
- I am not doing what God wants me to do with my life
- God does not love me
- God is angry at me
- God wants to punish me
- being judged by God
- being judged by God and then being found lacking

Stress Management and Time Issues:
The fear of / that:

- my stress will overwhelm me to the point where I become dysfunctional
- I cannot control my stress
- my stress may kill me or make me sick
- I do not have enough money or time
- I cannot control my life
- I am wasting money
- I am wasting my youth
- I am wasting time
- I do not know how to manage my stress
- others are the source of my stress and I cannot control them
- the future and what it holds
- not knowing the future
- moving forward with relationships or plans
- not having a goal
- not knowing what to do
- my choices of the past may catch up to me and cause me harm
- those I have hurt in the past may hurt me in the future
- being free of all that has encumbered me in the past

Trust Issues:
The fear of / that:

- I cannot trust those I love or depend upon
- I cannot trust or depend upon those I work with
- I cannot trust that my hard work will be rewarded
- I cannot trust my own mental or emotional decision-making
- I cannot trust or depend upon my own mind, body or emotional system
- I cannot trust my own thoughts, feelings or decision-making
- others cannot trust me and I cannot trust myself
- if others trust me then I will fail them
- if I trust others they will fail me
- others do not trust me
- others won't respond to me when I need them most
- the Universe really cares about me as an individual
- other people really care about me as a human being
- my spouse really loves me and that I can depend upon them

Victimhood:
The fear of / that:

- being victimized
- I am a victim
- I will always be a victim
- nothing I do will ever change what happened in the past
- others have more power than I do
- I don't have any power
- others are inherently bad people
- the world is full of bad people
- I can never be safe
- I can never protect myself
- I cannot protect my family or my children
- my children are not safe at school
- no one will protect me
- I can never regain my personal power and self-assurance
- everyone wants to hurt me
- others will think I am paranoid
- someone might kill me or murder me
- someone might rape me
- someone might want to hurt me or assault me
- someone will con me out of my finances
- physical assault or being robbed
- abuse of all kinds
- terrorists might attack my community

Vulnerability:
The fear of / that:

- being willing to accept help and support from others and showing my vulnerability in this process
- being completely defenseless and vulnerable
- being completely emotionally defenseless and vulnerable
- being overwhelmed or overcome by my fears
- I am being cheated by life or cheated out of my life and that life is fundamentally unfair
- being overwhelmed by information overload
- I do not really know who I am
- looking at life without fear and without being constantly "on guard"
- giving up every type of fear forever
- becoming that which I fear (example, that my fears will manifest in my life to my detriment)
- falling into old negative behaviors or patterns
- realizing what I am afraid of
- being too certain about anything and thus over confident
- being uncomfortable or in pain in any way
- missing out on an opportunity
- something bad could happen or is going to happen
- showing my emotions
- I will become what I hate most in others
- I will become what I fear most
- I am that which I fear
- I am never going to get all of my fears cleared
- being consumed by my fears
- conflict (whether it is family, relationship, political, financial, mental, physical, social, internal emotional, sexual, religious)
- asking for what I most want from others
- managing my personal space and boundaries
- losing my personal space or boundaries
- having my personal space or boundaries invaded
- vulnerability of all kinds (physical, emotional, sexual, financial, mental)
- my own weakness and appearing weak or vulnerable
- losing a job or being fired from a job
- not satisfying my partner whether emotionally financially or sexually
- being seen by others as non-confident
- not feeling confident enough to face life or relationship situations
- not understanding what is happening in my life
- wantonly enjoying life

Working with any of these statements that you emotionally resonate with can help free you from fear states that encumber your mind and decision-making processes. In later chapters we will discuss methods for working with and ultimately resolving all of them. No fear need define you, your life, your relationships or the results of your efforts.

Chapter 4: How Changes In Your Identity Create Fear:

An area of life that we fear greatly that is essential to understand is the loss of, or significant change in our perceived identity. As we live our lives, who we feel we are or perceive ourselves to be is always changing. These changes can be subtle or very dynamic and they occur from day-to-day. Our perceived identity is tightly woven into the fabric our families and of the society around us. It is also influenced by how others perceive us and by what experiences we have had in our lives and how we believe others have experienced us. Our identity is also made up of what society credits us with or judges us for, (i.e. Our educational degrees and our achievements as well as our indiscretions and prior judgments against us, whether they be legal judgments or social judgments, including seemingly minor ones such as negative gossip or criticisms).

This process of identity change, development and transformation across our lifetime can be exhilarating when positive or quite frightening when the changes are perceived negatively. In truth and spiritually speaking we are always at our core the "same person" throughout our lifetime. Yet who we perceive ourselves to be and who we want to be seen to be from an ego, ego self-defense and personality development perspective is always in a state of constant flux. Who others perceive us to be is also always changing, and it is always different from how we see ourselves to be. This difference of perspective about our identity and who we really are (how we see ourselves vs. how others see us) and our *inability to control it all* is a source of great fear for many of us. Therefore at a primal level most of us live in an ongoing state of fear of the loss of some aspect of our personal or social identity, social status, security and social power. We often do not realize these fears until we lose part of our perceived identity, status or power. Then we have a significant fear reaction and wonder how it all came about. Examples of this type of situation would be:

1. Having your financial identity or personal information stolen and misused
2. Having others unjustly see you in a negative light or being negatively gossiped about
3. Find out your spouse is having an affair and the change in how you feel about yourself that this brings
4. The change in social status you tend to feel if accused of committing a crime or that some of us feel for just receiving a speeding ticket
5. The change of status you feel when we lose a job, are demoted or are passed over for a promotion
6. Getting divorced or losing custody of your children

7. Losing your memory (and with it your perceived identity which you attach to your memories) from Alzheimers or dementia
8. Losing a major portion of your financial assets
9. Losing key relationships or experiencing a death in the family
10. Retiring or being placed in an assisted living facility
11. Moving to another country
12. Losing your house and all of your belongings in a fire or hurricane
13. Realizing that you have become addicted to a drug or alcohol
14. Realizing that your spouse or child has become addicted to a drug or to alcohol

Any of these fears can blindside us at any point in our lives. They live inside us until they are triggered by circumstance, unless we choose to face them proactively. That is what this book and the fear release processes in it are designed to do. To empower you to face and clear your fears before they take you over or detrimentally affect you at some later date. If you clear them now they will not affect your decisions, actions, mental processes, behaviors, relationships or life results. If it is worth it to you to face your fears and work through them I applaud you, if you choose not to I will respect your choice. We all have free-will and I respect yours. This process was designed to help you avoid pain and suffering, it is the "remove the band aid quick approach". In my personal experience, it brings far less discomfort than living with the fears and pains we all tend to carry year after year. I have personally had many of my own fears cleared very rapidly and watched many of my client's intense fears melt away in minutes. These were fears they had carried all their lives that had deeply affected their relationships or jobs.

I have done my best to describe the fear release processes in writing. Each person's emotional system functions slightly differently. If you are a very emotionally focused person they are likely to work very cleanly and directly for you. If you are a person who is highly intellectual and disassociated from your emotions, (i.e. always in your head, always thinking, very logic based, analytical, skeptical or who constantly tries to remain "rational" and to deny your emotions), they can still work great. I simply suggest you stay with the processes and give them a real chance; you and your emotional wellbeing are worth it.

For those of you who are mentally focused I suggest that you do not try to "figure out how the process works", do not try to think it through or analyze how it works. If you are skeptically minded, your fear driven skepticism can engage your fears and mental processes so much so that you are unwilling to simply recite a statement over and over, which is all you have to do with one of the release processes. If you try to think it through you will only be trying to apply your mind to your emotions. Which is like trying to have your mind "talk on" in an emotionally disconnected way, when it is better to be open to be listening quietly to your emotions. *You cannot think your way through an emotional process.*

I suggest that if you are a person who is very mentally focused that it is best if you just go with the instructions and give the process a chance. See how you feel in regard to the intensity of the fear you feel before applying the process and see how you feel after the process. If you feel discomfort or resistance while going through the process realize that it is likely that the parts of your system that have been holding onto your pain and your fear are simply resisting letting go. This is normal and natural and part of the process. Some people may have a brief feeling of slight intensification of the fear as they focus on it. This may be the first time in their lives that they have really focused on their fear, rather than trying to avoid it. When they do focus on their fear they may then realize just how pervasively it has been influencing their system. Still after this understanding occurs the fear then begins to process out. Any resistance generally passes very quickly as long as you keep focusing as per the instructions and continue reciting the statements as suggested. Realize that you are releasing old pain and fear as you recite the statement suggested. This may not initially be easy if your pain is great or your fear significant. Still it is good to let go of the past and necessary if you want to live in the present and to find your peace.

Chapter 5: "Catching Your Fears In Action":

Not all of us can feel our fears all the time, and many of us have blocked them out of our conscious minds completely. Often we can only feel our fears when they are triggered by certain circumstances, or in certain social or relationship situations. Even then we may not fully feel them. We may only feel stressed or may only feel muscular tension in our bodies, (for example our shoulders or neck muscles may tighten up) or we may notice a change in how we interact with other people. In very subtle situations we may only hear a slight change in our own voice tone or see slight changes in our behavior in certain situations or that we tend to avoid talking about certain subjects.

Therefore for us to become aware of some of our suppressed fears it may be necessary to monitor our own emotions during the day and to *learn to feel* when our fears are triggered by interactions with others or by specific situations. Then we can apply the fear clearing process in real time *at the moment we feel the fear.* We may also need to monitor how our bodies feel and sense when we "tense up" and/or feel stressed in order to begin to reflect upon our emotions in order to become aware of when we are actually afraid. Otherwise many of our fears will likely remain hidden and repressed and thus remain difficult to constructively address. Until we choose to become aware of our fears and actively map our hidden framework of fears they will remain obscured and tend to keep us imprisoned and limited. This need not be the case.

It is also important to realize that you can be just as afraid that something *will not happen in your life,* as you may be afraid that something *will happen.* When you are clearing your fears it is important to always look at both sides, *(or all sides),* of any issue, situation or relationship. Being willing to see all sides of your fears will empower you to clear all aspects of your fear of any situation. When you have accomplished this you are truly at peace with any situation or relationship and thus optimally empowered.

Consciousness is something that is developed, evolved and achieved over the course of a lifetime. It is also something that is achieved by methodically subtracting subconscious detrimental emotional dynamics and tendencies in a step by step manner. Being patient with yourself, tolerant of your imperfections and methodical in your process is essential. You, like all of us are a work in progress and eventually you will be a masterpiece.

Chapter 6: The "I Am My Fear" Technique For Clearing Fears:

1. Choose a fear that you want to permanently clear from your emotional system. It can be any fear that you have experienced, even if you have felt it all of your life.

2. Focus briefly upon the fear and do your best to understand and interpret the fear that you are feeling clearly, and in your mind form it into a clear simple verbal statement, such as the following. "I am afraid of being abandoned" or "I am afraid of heights" or "I am afraid of dying" or "I am afraid of failure" or "I am afraid of not being in control of my life".

   Realize that many people have a *string of fears* that they simultaneously fear, that may not appear rational at all, still this is what they do feel. This string of related fears acts like an emotional domino effect that can create an overwhelming reaction in their system. Therefore the entire list of fears must be cleared all at once in order for them to feel at peace. For example they may feel "I am afraid that my husband will betray me, leave me for another woman, and that I will then be alone forever and eventually die alone and penniless without children".

   If you have a string of fears that you envision, it is important that your chosen sentence include the entire string or "movie" of your fears, just as your emotional system fears they could occur. If you work with them in this way, then you can release them all simultaneously. For example a person could simultaneously have the fears: "I am afraid that my family members are going to hurt me, that they are all jealous of me, that they are intentionally cruel, and that they hate me, and that I am worthless and completely powerless to affect my situation". You can see that this is a situation where a person would feel trapped in the complex and seemingly unresolvable web of their fears of others, which could over time lead to aggression and depression as well as self-judgment. Aggression and depression are defined *here* as a maladaptive coping methods for unresolved and repressed *fear*. Often when people are aggressive it is simply that they fear others seeing their vulnerability and are trying to prove to others (and to themselves) that they are not vulnerable, although they truly feel *very vulnerable*.

3. Understand that this process of clearing your fear is not an intellectual process; it is a *completely emotional process, you cannot get there through your mind.* Fears need make no rational sense

whatsoever for them to affect your life, your relationships, your decisions and your emotions. That is why it is necessary for fear to be faced directly in order for it to be cleared. If you try to intellectualize this process of clearing your fears, think about it, or analyze it you will only get in your own way. So, it is good to "stay out of your mind" and *stay focused in your emotions* and feel your emotions as you do this work. "Just mouthing the words emotionlessly is not effective".

4. Close your eyes and focus on the *feeling of fear* you want to clear from your emotional system. Find the area in your body that you feel the fear the most. You may feel the fear (or feeling of tension or stress of the fear) in more than one area of your body. Such as in your solar plexus, or in your heart, throat or head; however there will usually be one place in your body that you feel it more than anywhere else. Focus on the core of this feeling in this area of your body as you perform the rest of the fear release process. If like some people, you feel the sensation of fear all over your body, do not worry, just focus all over as you recite the statement.

5. While remaining focused on the feeling of fear, wherever you actually feel it in your body, say the following statement out loud to yourself, (it still works even if you only say it silently to yourself, it is just better if you start out by actually speaking it out loud): "I AM MY FEAR OF …" Then add the description of what you are afraid of to the end of the sentence. For example if you are afraid of being abandoned you would say "I am my fear of being abandoned". DO NOT SAY, "I am *afraid* of being abandoned", as this will not work to clear the fear effectively. Also do not say "I am *in fear* of being abandoned".

   It is also useful to do your best to *put the feeling* of the emotion into your voice as you speak. Just mouthing the words tonelessly is not enough. You must move the "energy of the feeling" through your throat and express it with your voice to shift the energy most effectively and profoundly from where it has previously been stuck in your body. By saying "I am my fear", in effect you are directly facing your fear and acknowledging that your fear is nothing more than a manifestation of your own imagination and subconscious. This will break the well-worn habit of creating and projecting the fear outside of yourself. You are in effect consciously and willingly *owning* the emotion that you feel. This is necessary in any situation where you want to make effective progress in working with a detrimental emotion. Until you are willing to own your detrimental emotional states, reactions and relationship dynamics you cannot have power over them.

NOTE: The statement "I am my fear" is not a "negative affirmation". You are not giving yourself a "toxic affirmation or toxic energy" by reciting the statements. In fact your fears are already in your system, you simply haven't recognized them or processed them in the past. This technique simply *processes out* your own stuck toxic fear energy you have already been carrying without your realizing you have been carrying it. The process does not draw any new negativity to you. You will not become "lost in your fear" by reciting these statements, you will not be overwhelmed by them; this is a process of release.

It is important to realize that by saying the phrase "I am my fear of ..." you are *clearing fears*, you are not in any way validating your fear, reinforcing it, further identifying with it, becoming it, creating it in your future, magnifying it or "manifesting it from the universe". You are not saying that your fear is truly your "identity" as in your soul or who you are. You are saying that you are admitting that your fear is truly and only a part of your own energy system and that *you are finally willing to be self-accountable for that fact*, and nothing more than that. This realization is necessary in order to let it the fear go, and nothing more, once you fully accept this fact at all levels of your being the process is done. This acceptance is a powerful realization and an empowering willful choice. In fact it is an acceptance that through fearing you have *already been creating* that which you have feared in your life for quite a long time, without even realizing it. Fearing that you will harm yourself with your own fear energy is based on a sort of superstition, and is itself just another type of subconscious fear. I suggest that this fear can be released by using the statement "I am my fear of my fear" or "I am my fear that I can or am manifesting my fears". By stating this phrase you are realizing that what you have been afraid of is only an aspect of yourself, and nothing more and thus that you have nothing to be afraid of at all. If you fear using this technique you may wish to start out with the phrase "I am my fear of facing my fear" in order to overcome this initial emotional resistance.

6. Continue repeating the statement of "I am my fear of ..." over and over. As you do so focus on *speaking the words with the feeling of the emotion of fear in your voice that you are emotionally feeling* and focus on connecting with the emotion in your body where you feel it.

7. As you continue to repeat the statement you are likely to feel the energy and emotion of the fear begin to be somewhat more triggered than before, this is normal and to be expected and is part of the process. You may also feel various aspects of the emotion and your understandings of the situation it relates to that you had not previously noticed or realized begin to clear and release through various areas of your body. This is also normal and a necessary part of the process as these energies have previously been "stuck" in limiting states of understanding in various areas of your system.

   What you are experiencing is the process of those prior states of subconscious fear, pain and old recorded misperceptions of past experience releasing and shifting and processing out. Continue repeating the statement until you feel there is no more emotional releasing occurring and that your voice has gone sort of "flat", and that you are no longer engaged in the emotional release processing.

   When you first start, if the fear has a powerful emotional charge to it, it may be very hard to even say the words of the release statement for the first few times. It is necessary to push through this resistance, even if you feel some part of your emotions or internal dialog yelling "NO!". (This is a common experience by the way and it tends to pass quickly. Some people have strong resistance; some have almost no resistance and simply feel immediate relief.)

   As you continue to repeat the statement you may go through many different "phases" of release as different aspects of the fear release. An example would be where you have a non-specific or general fear of abandonment and you work with this process to release this fear. As you do so you may find that you are separately releasing fears of being abandoned by parents, friends, society in general, God, authority figures, and even from various aspects of yourself that have been in judgment of you. You may not know that you had these individual fears until you actually began to release the general fear of abandonment.

8. During the release of a fear it is common to have a sudden realization that there is an even deeper fear beneath it that you had not previously felt or understood to exist. For example, you may start out by working to release the fear of being judged or criticized by co-workers or your boss, and then find that you have a far deeper and more intense fear of failure that only surfaces once the original fear of criticism that you were previously aware of is cleared. If this is the case you can finish clearing the initial fear and then begin

clearing the underlying fear immediately afterward. It is fine to add on additional fear release statements dynamically as your fears arise.

9. Once you have completed the fear release process to your satisfaction, relax and evaluate how you feel about the fear that you initially started working with. How has it changed? How is it different than it was? Has its intensity diminished? Do you see the situation differently than you did when you started and if so in what ways? How will you now react differently to the situation that you were reacting to? If the fear was related to a relationship how do you feel differently about the relationship now? Some people find it beneficial to journal after release sessions. Journaling can give you an ongoing process and record of self-understanding and validation of your progress. Reading over you notes periodically can give you major insights into patterns and deeper understandings of self and relationship that are difficult to achieve in any other way.

10. If there is any emotional residue left of the fear in any part of your body focus on the core of the feeling in that part of your body and begin back at step 1. If the fear in that part of your body is in any way different, change your statement to fit the fear in that area of your body.

11. If you find that you have resistance to the release of any fear that you are working to release then all you need to do is focus on the feeling of resistance that you feel, wherever you feel it in your body and say to yourself, "I am my fear of releasing my fear" or "I am my fear of my fear" or "I am my resistance to releasing my fear". An example of this could be in the case of having fear of being fired. In this case if you have been reciting the statement "I am my fear of being fired" and the fear has not completely released then you can begin reciting the statement "I am my fear of releasing my fear of being fired".

12. It is also possible to have fear of fear and fear of being afraid and this can be released by saying "I am my fear of my fear". When we release fear energy it tends to move upward through our bodies, and this is a common sensation my clients report to me. Some people feel their fear energy release upward through their bodies very well as they recite the release statements until it seems to get a little stuck around the level of their chest. It is at this point that they can then use the statement that "I am my fear of my fear" or "I am my

resistance to releasing my fear" in order to release this last step in their fear processing.

A frequently asked question: How do I know when I am finished releasing my fear and that the fear I have been feeling is completely gone? Certainly if we no longer feel the fear we previously felt we can say we have gotten some relief from our prior fear. If we feel less anxiety, stress or body/muscle tension than we previously had this is also be a sign that our fear is reduced. Our fears also directly affect our interpretations of our lives, our relationships, our decisions and behaviors, the results of our choices and our moods. If we monitor how all of these have changed after the release work then we can begin to have assurance that we have successfully released our fears.

As our deepest core fears are released, one by one, we will tend to see positive changes in many areas of our lives. If you see changes in your ability to more effectively make decisions in your life where you were previously unable to make decisions or take action where you previously could not then you can be very sure your fears are diminishing. In the long run feeling increased relaxation, reduced stress, and increased feelings of empowerment and freedom are common results to look for. Keeping a personal journal can help you to more clearly realize the changes that have taken place in your system over time and to validate your efforts and to thereby inspire your future efforts and attainments.

4 Examples of How To Apply This Release Technique:

Scenario #1: A woman in a new relationship has problems with self-confidence and self-empowerment in terms of being able to speak openly to a boyfriend who is intimidating, verbally abusive and has threatened abandonment all at the same time. She has strong feelings and attraction for him; however she is not sure he is really good for her. This simultaneously brings up a combination of fears in the woman. This woman has a history of practicing meditation and yoga and so is very much in touch with her feelings and her body sensations of the stress she is feeling and can therefore focus on where she feels the sensations of fear as they process through her system in a real time manner. She tends to feel most of her feelings of emotional tension in the areas of her solar plexus and her heart.

Some of her fears are:

- Fear that she will lose a new and important love relationship
- Fear that she does not know how to make wise decisions in her relationship life
- Fear that she has made a mistake by dating this man in the first place
- Fear that she should have listened to her friends
- Fear that she is once again going to be hurt in a relationship
- Fear of being alone if she breaks up with him
- Fear of confronting him with the facts of his insensitive / abusive behavior
- Fear of escalation of the abusive behavior if she does confront the man
- Self-judgment and shame about having gotten involved in the relationship to begin with

This woman would apply the "I am my fear" release technique as described, first defining what her fears were, by writing down her fears and then writing out statements to recite in order to release each one. Since she has had practice with meditation and has awareness of her emotions and body she can focus on where she feels the emotional stress in her system (whether heart or solar plexus, depending upon the specific fear) as she recites the release statements.

Scenario #2: A man involved in a new relationship with a woman is torn between several contradictory emotions simultaneously. He is sure he loves the woman, is afraid of committing to the relationship due to past relationship problems and unresolved emotional wounds he had experienced. He also feels a deep conflict because both he and the woman want to be in control in the relationship. This man has no history of meditation, or self-introspection and is somewhat disassociated from his emotions and feels most of his negative emotions as physical tension in various parts of his body and a feeling of undefined tension in the area of his heart when his emotions are most triggered. He also feels his fear as tension in his shoulders and neck as well as tightness in his jaw muscles and forehead. He knows he feels fear and that it is affecting the relationship and his decisions; however he does not know how to work with it directly and is unsure how to tell if he is making progress. Although he is a very mentally focused individual, he is also very visually inclined and whenever he feels his fears, if he closes his eyes, he pictures his fears as a dark cloud hanging over his life.

His fears are:

- Fear of commitment
- Fear of abandonment
- Fear of being hurt again
- Fear of appearing weak or non-dependable if he is unwilling to commit
- Fear of appearing dishonest if he does not communicate his emotions clearly and directly
- Fear of talking about his past relationships because he does not want to look wounded or dysfunctional
- Fear of talking about his past relationships because he does not want to create jealousy, comparison, arguments or unnecessary drama in a new and as yet uncommitted relationship
- Fear of looking like he does not have his emotional act together
- Fear that he is not yet ready for a new and committed relationship
- Fear that he cannot handle a woman who wants to either share equally in all decisions in the relationship or even more fear producing, a woman who may be stronger than he is and who may at times "push him around"
- Fear that he may be deeply hurt if he has to give up the relationship or mishandles the situation, because he does truly love the woman

In order for this man to work through his emotions it is helpful for him to repeat the fear statements that most directly process his fears, such as "I am my fear of being hurt again in a relationship", while focusing on the areas of tension in his body, until the areas of tension release and relax. He can also work with his fears while focusing on the visualization of the dark cloud in his mind's eye until he either sees it dissolve fully or change into a more positive image. In this kind of situation it is best for the man to simply continue working with the practice of reciting the statements, even if he cannot initially "feel it working", since it is common for people using this process to have emotions open up spontaneously that have previously been shut down, numbed, stuck or blocked even if they feel nothing at first. When this opening of emotions occurs he may be able to begin to feel fears that he had previously not felt safe feeling, which although it is simply *feeling his feelings of fear* is actually progress. This can be the start of a far more comprehensive process of becoming more emotionally self-aware and interactively functional and capable of intimacy in his relationship. This man also has constant internal dialogs going on of "doing this work is stupid and a waste of time", "I should be able to control my emotions", "feeling my fears will only mean I am weak". These types of internal blocking statements are normal and tend to get in the way of being willing to feel and then release our fears and negative emotions *if we choose to listen to them* instead of continuing with the release process. They are simply representative of our instinctive fear of releasing our fears by creating rationalizing dialog for not facing our fears. It is best to ignore the dialog and continue with the practice until the dialog itself processes out.

Scenario #3: A single parent with few financial resources is raising four children. One of her teenage daughters is constantly involved with problem boyfriends, is creating problem social networking situations, has exhibited a high potential for drug abuse and is unwilling to communicate with her mother. There are constant arguments and no real substantive communications between mother and daughter on what the true nature of the problem is. The parent feels many fears and insecurities and is torn, not knowing which direction to go or how to make decisions in regard to the relationship with her daughter, and her various fears are paralyzing her into non-action. This woman has no history with meditation, yoga, counselling or therapy of any kind; however she is very much in touch with her fear unhappy emotions and feels them in different parts of her body. Each different fear state and other negative emotion is felt in a different specific part of her body, including in her head, her throat, her heart, her stomach and even in her feet.

Her fears are:

- Fear that if I constrain or criticize my child too much she may act out more dramatically than in the past, just to prove she can
- Fear that if I don't set clear boundaries my child won't make wise decisions and will get into even more trouble
- Fear that my child will hate and abandon me emotionally if I push them too hard or try too hard to control them
- Fear that I cannot reach my child no matter what I do

- Fear that my child is growing away from me and shutting down emotionally
- Fear that I may lose my connection with my child if I mishandle the relationship
- Fear that I fundamentally do not understand my child
- Fear that my lack of success working with my daughter means I am a bad mother
- Fear that my daughter's negative actions and behavior means that I have failed as a mother
- Fear that I do not understand what is going on or how to handle it
- Fear that there may be no solution to all of the problems we are going through
- Fear that my child may get pregnant
- Fear that my child may be having sex and I don't know it
- Fear that my child may be taking drugs and I don't know it
- Fear that my child might overdose on drugs
- Anger toward my child for creating these problem situations
- Hatred toward myself for not being a better mother and solving the problems
- Guilt and shame for failing as a mother

For this woman focusing on the specific feeling that she feels in her body that she associates with the specific fear that she is working on at the moment is her best option. Then working "fear by fear" she can clear the fears and each separate emotional charge that is located in each area of her boy until they are all resolved. She can also use the release statements listed in Chapter 7 to release her feelings of sadness, hatred, guilt and shame as they only undermine the effectiveness of her managing the relationship with her daughter.

Scenario #4: A man is suffering from a form of PTSD (Post Traumatic Stress Disorder) after the traumatic death of his mother and the incomplete grieving process that he went through in regard to her passing 25 years in the past. The sudden accidental and violent death of his mother when he was very young created a situation of un-faced and therefore unprocessed and unresolved fears and emotional traumas, which the man had never really worked through. His instinctive reaction to his pain and loss had been to suppress his fears and numb himself to the pain at a time when he had not been self-aware enough to understand how to grieve the loss, nor had the tools or methods to work through the trauma. His subconscious feelings of fear of her death and dying were in a sense "frozen in time" in his emotional system, twenty five years in the past, in an incompletely processed form, which then blocked him emotionally in his other relationships later in life. Only 25 years later did the old fears surface to a level that he could become consciously aware enough of them to effectively work with them.

These "parts of his emotional system" were not fully in awareness of and in acceptance of the fact that his mother had actually died and therefore he had never completely grieved her death. Because of this situation he has been unable to establish heathy loving relationships in the present, because these parts of his system are "literally stuck in and living in the past". Up until this point he has been unaware of why he has had problems forming committed relationships. This emotional blockage led to various negative controlling dynamics in his dating relationships and a fear of commitment and therefore he never married. Paradoxically he is NOW experiencing the fears listed below as if it were twenty five years ago and is somewhat confused as to why he is having these feelings surface, since he assumed he had "dealt with" his loss years ago:

- I fear my mother dying
- I fear losing my mother forever
- I fear facing life without my mother in my life
- I fear that I was not there when she needed me the most
- I fear that I should have been there for her
- I fear that I will never get over this pain and loss
- I fear that a part of me is dying too
- I fear that there is nothing I can do to help her and that *it is all my fault*

This man had not allowed himself to feel these fearful feelings years before and it has taken 25 years for them to surface on their own after having created numerous relationship issues due to their repression. Of course the original situation of his mother's passing was an accident and had nothing to do with him, still it is common for loved ones to blame themselves when those they love are hurt or die. In this case he blamed himself for not having been there when she needed him, even though based on the facts of the situation that was logically not possible.

Working through each of the fears with an "I am my fear" statement can allow the stuck emotional energy to be released and allow this portion of the man's grieving process to be completed. Once these fears have been cleared there are then other steps in the emotional grieving process that can be worked through that were not possible due to the fear blockages. Eventually full acceptance of the pain, loss and trauma will allow the man to be emotionally open to the present and to relationships without fear of the pain of such loss reoccurring in the future in some other form, (i.e. fearing the potential death or abandonment of the woman he chooses to marry).

In each of these described scenarios there are several fears or negative emotions that must all be addressed if progress is to be made in the relationship or the person's life. In many cases these fears and emotions must be addressed rapidly or even *simultaneously* if the person involved wants to attain positive or optimal results. This is a key reason that fear release and negative emotional release techniques are beneficial to relationship management and management of our ongoing emotional processes. Once the fears are addressed each person described in each scenario is in a far better emotional situation. They tend to feel more centered, grounded, empowered, emotionally at peace and self-confident in terms of making wise decisions that are in their own best interest, as well as in the best interest of those they love. In essence they are better prepared to see their situation more clearly and without the filters that their fears and negative emotions have been creating.

Chapter 7: The Special Case of Clearing Feelings of Hatred:

We have all hated someone or some situation, and oddly enough we may have even hated some aspect of ourselves, including our behavior, our own emotional process, our appearance or past decision-making. Up until this point in human history this has been accepted as a "normal" part of the human experience, however this need not continue. This type of situation is unnecessary and can be directly reconciled with the methods in this book. It is simply human to feel hatred; it is not evil, wrong or bad. If you cannot accept that you do feel hatred, then you cannot be willing to heal it from your system and transcend its effects forever. Self-forgiveness is the best first answer to feelings of hatred, because we are then empowered to clear it from our systems. It is the *self-judgment of hatred* that keeps it stuck in our systems.

The suggested way to address hatred is to first consciously recognize that you feel the feeling of hatred, whatever the reason, even if it is toward yourself, without any judgmentalness at all for having felt the emotion. Simply determine who or what you hate. Then choose to accept and forgive yourself for feeling the emotion. Then formulate a sentence, just as you did when you were determining what you were afraid of in the Process for Clearing Fear in Chapter 6. When you have determined who or what you are feeling hatred toward, use the same technique, except exchange the words "I am my fear of / that ..." with the words "I am my hatred of ..." while focusing on your feelings of hatred wherever you feel them most in your body. Continue repeating the phrase until the feeling of hatred has completely processed out of your system.

Some example release phrases would be:

- I am my hatred of being out of control
- I am my hatred of being controlled by others
- I am my hatred of other's tendencies to control me
- I am my hatred of feeling powerless and vulnerable
- I am my hatred of my own weakness
- I am my hatred of my addiction
- I am my hatred of being overweight or the way I look
- I am my hatred of the way I feel others see me
- I am my hatred of myself for what I did
- I am my hatred of Bill for firing me
- I am my hatred of Sue for divorcing me and taking the children
- I am my hatred of Frank for betraying me and having an affair

- I am my hatred of my best friend for lying to me and stabbing me in the back

Yes, the process does require you to fully accept and admit (rather than deny and suppress) your feelings of hatred of self and others. Once you do admit that you do feel this undesirable feeling and that a part of you "is" this feeling of hatred, which is just an intense reaction to the fear and pain you feel or have felt in the past, it goes away. You will not become "more hateful" by stating that you are your hatred. You will not draw negative energy to you by saying these statements. You will not be *socially wrong or bad* for having admitted your hatred. You will become *less hateful* because you will process it out of your system by consciously acknowledging your emotion and therefore cease to suppress and cease to hold this negative energy in your system, and it will cease to fester in a repressed state in your subconscious. In effect you will bring to bear all of your conscious loving abilities to manifest a new and more conscious and positive interpretation of whoever it is that you have been hating by this process. You will do this instead of holding onto the old fearful and often misguided prior mis-interpretation. *It is your judgmentalness of the wrongness of feeling this emotion that keeps you from acknowledging that you feel it in the first place, and this self-judgment keeps the hatred stuck in your system.* Releasing the self-judgment of it being "wrong or socially unacceptable to feel hatred" allows you to peacefully work through the emotion and to ultimately release it from your system, and thus be free of it forever. *You can forgive yourself* for feeling hatred and thus cease to feel hatred.

It is not wrong to feel hatred; it is simply human; it is not useful to hold onto this feeling of hatred for one more second than it takes to process it out of your system. Hatred is a feeling of fearful vulnerability and powerlessness and anger and judgmentalness and is the primal desire to destroy that which we feel threatened by. It is not wrong to be afraid and to want to protect oneself, and I do not suggest judging fear itself or other fearful people for being afraid. It is however not optimal, healthy or wise to use the emotion of hatred to protect oneself. There are far better and more conscious, constructive and positive ways to accomplish this goal that are *not* driven by negative emotion. This is why it is better to release this energy than to either hold onto it, rationalize it, or to act upon it.

When we are in a state of hatred or negative judgment of ourselves or others we often do not want to forgive. The reason that we do not want to forgive others or ourselves is always because in some part of our being we do not feel safe doing so, or it feels "wrong to do so" and therefore unsafe to do so. Therefore the reason we do not feel *safe* forgiving self or others is because at some level of our systems we *fear doing so* for some reason. This reason may be conscious or it may be subconscious and we can release this fear. If we recognize the fear that is driving our hatred or our judgmentalness and release it then we can find it within ourselves to forgive those we are in judgment of and even those that we openly hate. We can even choose to forgive ourselves, which is sometimes the most difficult act of forgiveness. Therefore if we want to forgive, fear must first go. Forgiveness is always worth doing, if not for others, for our own state of inner peace and spiritual development, and in truth it is a gift to the whole world. Hatred is not in alignment with Spirit / God, God is love.

I have no judgement of any human state or emotion. Judging emotions only creates *a sort of attachment to them* and therefore gets them endlessly stuck in our systems. Self-judgment does not lead to negative emotions being released or resolved, you cannot judge away hatred or other negative emotions. Only by releasing self-judgments of our emotions can we release them from our systems and be free of negative emotions. I do perceive some emotional states to be more advantageous and wise than others. I do perceive love, joy, inner peace and happiness to be far more advantageous and optimal than fear, anger or hatred.

There are several other negative of dysfunctional emotional states one can feel toward self and others that can also be released with this technique and which are difficult to face or release in any other way. These are feelings of:

- Shame and Guilt
- Self-disgust
- Self-distain
- Self-loathing
- Self-revulsion
- Self-pity
- Feeling sorry for oneself

For these states the same process can be applied as in:

- I am my feeling of shame or guilt
- I am my feeling of self-disgust
- I am my feeling of self-distain
- I am my feeling of self-loathing, etc.

In regard to working with negative feelings towards others, you would use statements to clear these states, such as:

- I am my hatred of Bill
- I am my loathing of Sue
- I am my feeling of revulsion for Kevin

It is important to understand that these intense negative emotional states can reside in all of us, whether towards ourselves or others. If we do not choose to recognize them, they will continue to affect us and others without our knowledge and to our detriment. If we do choose to courageously acknowledge them and address them directly we can quickly transcend them and live life without the influence, limitations and pain they continue to create in our lives. It is simply a choice we have the option of making at any moment of our lives. It is a choice that can ultimately offer us inner peace and peace in our relationships, or it can keep peace from us, and those we have the potential to love more fully.

Chapter 8: Identifying & Clearing Your Larger Framework of Fears, Beliefs and Expectations:

Below are some example clearing statements to get you started in your process of clearing your system of fears. Some people begin clearing their fears and have good success at first and then stop, without consciously understanding exactly why they have chosen to do so, rather than following through with the process for the long term. In this situation, their subconscious fears have undermined their fear release process without their realizing that this has happened. Meaning that they fear releasing their fears because they feel unsafe doing so. They feel unsafe because they instinctively feel their fears are what is keeping them safe. Therefore it is the process of *actually succeeding in releasing their fears* that causes them to become afraid *in a new way* and to stop releasing their fears. This potential situation can be overcome by setting a clear conscious intention and personal commitment to continue a reasonable daily practice of release work, and continuing to clear a few fears each day for an extended period of time. Journaling will help you to validate your progress and successes. In this way you can move forward gradually, not pushing your emotional system any faster or farther than you are ready to move.

Example Clearing Statements:

- I am my fear of being alone / overweight / weak / ugly / stupid
- I am my fear of not being able to stop drinking, smoking, taking drugs, etc.
- I am my fear of others hating me
- I am my fear of others abandoning me
- I am my fear of others rejecting me
- I am my fear of others controlling me
- I am my fear of death and/or dying
- I am my fear of (add the specific illness or debilitated state you fear)

At this point you can now refer to and work with any of the fear topics listed previously that you marked off in Chapter 3's "Master Reference List of Fears" and create your own statements specifically tailored to your own life situation and set of experiences. If you want to more fully understand your own system of subconscious beliefs, values, expectations, emotional processes and ways you manage your boundaries in relationships there are also four additional self-assessment work sheets at the end of this book that you can work with. These self-assessment exercises can help you raise your subconscious fears to the surface of your consciousness so that you can effectively work with them and resolve them permanently. These exercises can also help you to focus in on what you actually do fear and what dysfunctional beliefs you have so that you can re-work your whole system of life decision-making strategies and how you manifest your life goals from the ground up, if this is your desire. In addition, if you have fears you have not previously been able to understand these exercises can help you bring them into focus so that you are more empowered to deal with what have in the past been non-specific or undefined states of fear, anxiety, stress or worry.

Fears and beliefs that remain subconscious may simply continue to affect your life and your relationships to your detriment without your realizing their effect. You now have the power, the methods and the options to change all of these emotional situations and their effects on your life for the better. If you work through these exercises you are likely to learn a great deal about yourself as well as how you relate to others and how you see yourself, others, life, the world and your closest relationships. You will also gain a great deal of insight into how you make decisions which then will give you the opportunity to change your decision-making processes for the better should you choose to. These exercises are listed in the back of the book in the section marked Appendix to Chapter 8 as:

- Emotional Self-Analysis
- Belief System Analysis
- Values / Priorities Assessment Worksheet
- Emotional and Relationship Boundary Mapping Exercise

You now have a robust and comprehensive system you can apply to understand yourself and your relationships better and that you can effectively work with. With these tools you can resolve the larger framework of fears and framework of expectations and fear based beliefs that have likely been keeping you from having many wonderful life experiences and relationship situations that you have desired. It is important to have and to maintain a positive perspective as you dismantle your system of fears and to realize your power in this process. Freedom from fear is possible and you deserve it.

Chapter 9: Releasing Negative Emotions, Judgmentalness & Our Hidden Prejudice:

The process for clearing fears from Chapter 6 can also be used to directly clear other negative emotions such as shame and guilt. It can be used in the form of "I am my shame" or "I am my guilt" or "I am my depression" to relieve these states. In situations of very deep pain or self-dislike you may find the benefit of using the statement "I am my self-loathing". In addition, if you cannot actually pinpoint or name the painful emotion you are feeling, you may wish to voice the simple statement "I am my pain".

Another way to work with this statement to clear other negative feeling states about oneself or towards others is by repeating the statement "I am my feeling of / that ...". An example of this would be, "I am my feeling that I am a bad person" or "I am my feeling that I deserve a miserable life". Additionally you can use this to clear feelings such as panic, worry or anxiety as in "I am my feeling of panic" or "I am my feeling of anxiety" or "I am my feeling of worry". This method works to process out any negative feeling state.

It is often not easy to actually voice these types of feelings about ourselves, even privately to ourselves. However, if you can simply bring yourself to do so, and bear the temporary discomfort of doing so, then the stuck emotions can be freed from your system, processed out, and you can leave them behind for good. If you use this technique and the emotions still feel incompletely released I would suggest trying the statements "I am my resistance to releasing the feeling that I am ...", as in "I am my resistance to releasing the feeling that I am a bad person" or "I am my resistance to releasing my feelings of hatred" or "I am my resistance to releasing my feelings of panic".

It is useful to realize that just as we try to hold onto fear we also sometimes try to hold onto anger, guilt, shame, etc. and we can overcome this tendency with statements such as "I am my *resistance* to releasing my shame". If you cannot get in touch with the *underlying fear* that is driving these surface feelings it can help to use these statements in order to "get past or out of" these more conscious and debilitating emotional states. Doing so may help you "right yourself" emotionally and give you the confidence and emotional balance to then delve into the underlying fear that you also want to clear. Again the reason that we feel negative emotions of all kinds is that we have recorded misunderstandings in our memory at subconscious levels about life, self and relationships. This process of reciting these statements helps by raising the energy of those subconscious memories and associated emotions into our higher consciousness where they can be successfully reprocessed and understood in new and more constructive ways.

Oddly enough, because there is such a tight connection between being judgmental toward someone and fearing them at subconscious levels, a process similar to "I am my fear" can also help clear judgmentalness. You can do this by saying "I am my judgment of ..." as in "I am my judgment of my boss" or "I am my judgment of my husband/wife" or "I am my judgment of terrorists". If one works with these types of statements, we can help process out the energy of our buried fear, as well as our hatred, resentment, animosity, and even *prejudice and stereotypes* in regard to our relationships with these people. This can be a process by which those of us who realize that they have unwanted *subconscious prejudice* toward other nations, races, religions or cultures can effectively and rapidly reduce their tendency to hold onto this prejudice. It can be a process by which we release our bias's and our *projected stereotypes* and begin to see the unique and wonderful human beings that are standing before us, rather than the projected stereotypical memory of what we have learned or been taught to see others as.

It is interesting to note that being judgmental about or toward the concept of judgmentalness is itself a way of being judgmental. We cannot judge judgmentalness away, just as we cannot resent away resentment or hate away hatred. Judgmentalness, resentment and hatred are all driven by underlying fears. If you want to lose your tendency to judge yourself or others for being judgmental you can use the following statements. "I am my judgment of my judgmentalness" or "I am my judgment of my tendency to judge myself or others" or "I am my judgment of others tendency to be judgmental". You can even use the statement "I am my hatred of those who hate me".

Recent studies have shown that even people who consciously consider themselves to hold no conscious prejudice or stereotypes at all toward other genders, sexual orientations, races, religions or cultures often do hold *subconscious negative bias* that they are completely unaware of. Further it has been shown that these subconscious biases actually directly affect their behaviors and decisions toward the groups they are unconsciously prejudiced toward without their realizing it. This type of subconscious effect explains much in regard to the inequality that many people in the world experience, including the dismissive way the poor are often treated. I would say that all of us have the potential to have some subconscious prejudice, bias or judgmentalness of some sort, *because we all have a subconscious*.

The process of stereotyping people is a process very similar to prejudice, in that it draws upon a set of often subconscious and usually negative beliefs we hold about a group of people, and causes us to project those beliefs onto our mind's eye as we interact with these people. Our projection in effect literally "overwrites" the person we are seeing right in front of us and thus distorts what they are saying and doing and therefore creates *misinformation and misinterpretations in our own systems*. When this happens we begin making decisions based upon this misinformation, as if it were true and accurate, and as if the information came from the outside environment around us, rather than just from our subconscious memory. In effect this is a process of projecting our subconscious expectations from our own memories that we have unknowingly associated with specific groups of people.

We tend not to question the accuracy or authenticity of this misinformation we have presented to ourselves. When this process is engaged it happens so fast and so unconsciously that we do not notice it is even occurring. If you question that this process happens in your own system, just listen carefully to your thoughts, emotional reactions and internal dialog that come up in your system when you visualize different ethnic groups, religious groups, people in prison, or people of a different sexual orientation. It is likely that you will immediately be assailed by a lot of thoughts or feelings in regard to who they *supposedly* are, what they are *supposedly* like, what traits they *supposedly* have, how they *supposedly* will behave or think and how interactions with them would *supposedly* go. All of this is false information of course, in that no individual person tends to function in the way we stereotypically assume a group of people would. I would also suggest that any stereotype we have of any group of people is probably significantly inaccurate. Lumping human beings into groups of characteristics and then judging them for those characteristics may simplify life, yet it is dehumanizing and ultimately detrimental to all of us.

Most of us hold stereotypes today about many groups of people, including children, old people, the poor, the rich, Americans, Jews, Islamists, Russians, blacks, Italians, Catholics, Hispanics, gays (male and female), Asians, etc.. All of these stereotypes diminish and limit our ability to accurately see the individuals we interact with who are members of these groups. We are in effect constantly deluding our own process of interpreting our interactions with them and thereby creating new *false memories* of our experience with these individuals, which we then refer to in the future as food for further stereotyping. Each of our recorded *stereotypes* are, as described earlier in this book, an *expectation that we hold about the world and other people. We expect individuals to act like our stereotypical expectations of the groups they belong to.* Then when our subconscious expectations are not met we feel *fear and anxiety, and this fear then can even motivate us to subconsciously push these people to meet our negative expectations and thus to act like the stereotypes we hold in our minds.*

In essence we literally try to motivate individuals we meet, through our expectations, to act like the stereotypes we hold, and if they do not do so we feel uncomfortable and even somewhat stressed. They feel our expectations at subconscious levels and realize that if they do not meet our expectations that they, in a way, risk our social abandonment, judgment and punishment. In essence if they fail to act in the dysfunctional ways that we expect them to, then we will reject them for it. Therefore we subconsciously very much want our stereotypes to be "true", so that we can feel more *in control* of our world, and thus feel *safe*, even when we are totally *wrong for wanting this.* What does this process of trying to make our stereotypes true in the outside social world just so that we can feel safe mean for those who inforce the law? For educators at all levels of the educational system? For judges? For parents who are raising children? For managers of businesses? For those who make laws? For those who govern nations? All of these people are to some degree being motivated by their fear of individuals not fitting their stereotypical molds, and are motivated to get those people to fit their molds, or to ignore any information that does not support their stereotypes. This is a serious issue if these people are in positions of authority, influence, powerful decision-making and have the ability to affect many other people's lives.

I have not seen any studies of how the very wealthy subconsciously regard the middle class or the poor, yet I feel that such studies would be very enlightening. The world can no longer endure such subconscious "masked", detrimental and undermining tendencies. In these situations I would suggest working with the statement "I am my prejudice toward or of…" or "I am the stereotypes I hold in regard to …" and then fill in the blank with whichever group(s) you feel you may potentially hold any subconscious prejudice or stereotypes toward. In cases of stereotyping you could work with the statement "I am my fear and judgment of this person for not meeting my expectations of them". If you have fear of any group of people, and do not know specifically why you do so, you can simply recite "I am my fear of ….". If you have hatred of any group of people you can simply recite the statement "I am my hatred of ….".

If you do have any subconscious prejudice or hold any stereotypes, it is likely that you will feel the energy of the release begin moving through your body soon after you begin reciting these phrases. I can assure you that the world will be far better off without these tendencies.

Chapter 10: Vulnerability Is Your Greatest Power:

Most people fear either feeling or being vulnerable in any way, and see it only as a state of weakness and potentially being open to being hurt, attack or destruction. This is especially true of many males who are often taught to always be on their guard, always be "in the know", always have the "right answer", always be in control, or always be hyper-competitive and remain dominant at all costs. Unfortunately many women are also finding that in order to compete in the corporate world today that functioning in a similar way to men is *supposedly* a useful competitive strategy. They are being taught by the competitive environment to avoid emotional vulnerability at all costs and to even judge and demean the state of vulnerability publically. *Some* deeply emotionally wounded women have even defensively resorted to the traditionally male tactic of bullying. I would suggest that all of these offensive reactions to *fear of vulnerability* are just that, fear reactions, and not a true expression of any power or wisdom at all. It has never been a true sign of power or wisdom for either men or women to function in this way. *Emotional vulnerability is power*, emotional openness is power, and loving kindness is true power. This is true because emotional vulnerability requires *emotional self-awareness* and self-awareness is an empowered state. Fortunately for all of us most women are usually better at realizing this sooner than most men.

This process of trying to manage one's fears by controlling the social environment, and managing one's emotions by controlling away one's fear of vulnerability does not make fear go away. In fact it further entrenches it deeper into the subconscious and lends further credence to the misapprehension that there is actually something to be afraid of. This is of course fundamentally disempowering. I would suggest that there is a more conscious and optimal route to addressing life's issues and even the threatening situations we sometimes face in life. People who are constantly wrapped up in trying not to be vulnerable are also constantly wrapped up in ego self-defense mechanisms and fear reaction dynamics. They are so busy trying to make sure that they are "safe" that they have forgotten how to be open and receptive to life, their emotions, other's emotions, and to relax and let life and love in. Therefore they are constantly in "fear projection mode" and worst case scenario mode, rather than seeing what really is going on, either within themselves or in others.

For anyone who is constantly trying to be in control and be safe, vulnerability can be terrifying, and they may only get there when all of their ego self-defense mechanisms have first failed. In this situation they may feel totally naked and defenseless. Only at this point are they finally able to make their first consciously aware decision, because only at this point have they stopped projecting their subconscious fears onto the world. It is a harsh way to learn the value of vulnerability; still it is a way that many of those who are deeply entrenched in fear choose. No one can control their lives because each of us, and everyone else, have free-will. We all must therefore learn how to be vulnerable at some point if we want to get emotionally close to others, even if it means learning it at the moment of our own deaths.

I would suggest starting by redefining the word vulnerability. In my personal definition of vulnerability I start by taking the words fear, safety, control, attack and destruction out of the definition entirely, and I replace them with "expansive loving conscious *fearless* openness to and awareness of all that is". I would also suggest that fully surrendering to God is a great way to learn to become more vulnerable. In this state you are not projecting anything, you are living completely in the now and you are open to whatever may happen. This does not mean that you are unwilling to defend yourself; it means that if you choose to do so you will not do so from fear or anger, you will do so from consciously understanding the benefit or necessity of doing so. You will not be *reacting*, you will be *consciously responding* to your environment. Vulnerability means having your heart and mind open in a loving way to everyone at all times, even if they are hateful and cruel, because this is the most powerful way you can meet anyone. If you meet hatred with love you have the potential to heal it and to understand it and transcend it into love and to resolve any conflict. If you meet hatred with hatred you only create more hatred and limit your options.

Vulnerability means being open to do whatever it takes to achieve *full understanding* of whomever or whatever you are interacting with or dealing with, including yourself. It is a fiercely courageous state of love and compassion for everyone and everything. It is a willingness to acknowledge one's own constant ignorance and to realize our need to learn from every moment of life and relationship. It is egoless unconditional love and compassion. It is powerful, and it is never powerless. It does not come from a place of supposed knowing. It comes from a place of wanting and being willing to know, to understand and to help, no matter what the cost. Vulnerability is your greatest power, because without it you cannot learn anything worth knowing and if you do not learn what vulnerability can teach you, how can you help those you love or the world that needs so very much what only you have to offer it?

Vulnerability is the essence of intimacy, and for those who want true intimacy in their lives this is the path you have been looking for. For all of us, in our deepest emotional being, we want to be fully accepted and fully wanted, and we cannot achieve this if we are afraid of it occurring or defending against it. Therefore we must release our fear of abandonment and rejection, as well as release our fear of not being wanted and not being accepted. Working with the following statements can help:

- I am my fear of being emotionally vulnerable
- I am my fear of emotional intimacy
- I am my fear of not being wanted
- I am my fear of being rejected
- I am my fear of being abandoned
- I am my fear of not being fully accepted
- I am my fear of my own emotional decision-making
- I am my fear of making emotional decisions that can hurt me
- I am my fear of being hurt if I get too close to someone else
- I am my fear of loving too much
- I am my fear of allowing others to get too close to me

I wish you all the best in your quest for intimacy, love and empowered vulnerability.

Chapter 11: Release Statements For Those On The Spiritual Fast Track:

There are those of us who are striving to attain spiritual consciousness rapidly. If you are one of these people you may find that you consistently fall back into fear, anger, judgmentalness, sadness and negative emotions of various kinds. This tendency does not of course support the attainment of higher consciousness or of retaining it once attained. If you are a person of higher or spiritual consciousness you may also have the difficulty of becoming or remaining "grounded". The state of not being grounded tends to say that we have subconscious unresolved fear of some sort, though we may not know what it is associated with. These fears can be related to not feeling safe in the world, or not feeling safe in our relationships with others, or with society and they can all be cleared.

The following statements can help us open to spirit.

I am my fear:

- that I am unworthy of God's love
- of completely surrendering to God in all aspects of my life
- of living in complete gratitude to God in all aspects of my life for the rest of my life
- of asking God for forgiveness for everything that I have said, done, thought or felt
- of hearing or receiving spiritual guidance in every moment of my life
- of actually hearing my spirit guides guidance, and of how my life may be changed by doing so
- of completely seeing, comprehending and understanding myself, the world and God
- of placing my relationship with God above all other considerations, values and relationships in my life
- of completely aligning all aspects of my being, mind, body, emotions, and spirit with God at all times, forever
- of completely resonating with God in all aspects and levels of my being, including mind, body, emotions and spirit at all times, forever
- that God will not forgive me for all of the wrong that I have done in the past
- that God will not completely forgive, accept and love me
- that I am so spiritually or emotionally tainted, broken or damaged that I am incapable of being fully resonant with God and accepted by God

The following statements can help us to become more consciously grounded:

I am my fear:

- of not being safe in the world
- of not being safe with my family
- of not being safe where I live
- of not being accepted by others
- of being rejected by others
- of being harmed by others
- of being one with humanity
- of not being accepted by the universe
- of being fully accepted by the universe
- of not being safe with and accepted by those I love
- of being hurt if I connect with others
- of not being able to trust others
- of not being able to trust myself
- that I do not know how to connect fully with others in a healthy way
- of being hurt if I connect with the world and humanity

I wish you well on your spiritual journey.

Chapter 12: The Power of Gratitude, Your Road to Joy and Inner Peace:

Looking at life through the eyes of gratitude first and always is not initially easy, still it is always rewarding. My suggestions in regard to gratitude may not be what you are used to, in that I suggest being grateful for *everything in your life*, and yes I do mean even being grateful for all of the pain you have endured in your life. I do mean being grateful for the traumas, the heartaches, the illnesses and the losses. This may seem to be a terrible statement. I hope not.

In my work I have met people who have endured experiences that are terrible beyond description or imagining. Their lives and their sufferings are private and I will not describe them here. What I have learned in my work is that they have all grown tremendously and powerfully from what they have lived through. I have seen them become great, wise, beautiful and wonderful people from these challenges. I personally believe in God and believe that there are always reasons, often beyond our understanding, for the problems and challenges we face in life. We often do not see the reasons for our trials or understand their benefits until long after we have experienced them.

I believe that we grow, learn and evolve from every free-will choice we make and every life experience we are blessed to have. I also believe that all lives, even painful lives, are given by God and that there must be some useful reason for them, if we are only willing to look for it. I am not suggesting a "Pollyanna" approach to life or dismissing anyone's painful life experiences as trivial. I am only suggesting that constructively and positively managing our perspective in regard to how we look at our lives means everything in how we deal with our challenges. If we can learn to consciously manage our perspective on life and how we interpret our life experience then our emotional state becomes manageable. Our emotional state is a direct reflection (for better or worse) of our interpretation of our life experiences, our relationship experiences and thus of the *memories we have chosen to record.*

Over and over I have seen people muster their courage and attain amazing insights from the challenges they have faced and ultimately risen above. Whatever you have experienced in life, however wrong it may have seemed, I personally believe that there is something positive and useful that you will gain from it. Though it may not in any way be obvious in the moment, and although it probably won't be what you expect to learn or gain. I have complete faith in this, otherwise I would not and could not make this statement, and would not trivialize your pain by being trite or offering you false promise or hope. I have shared the pain of those I work with day after day, and done my best to feel and understand their situations as much as I could. Of course I did not fully experience or understand their pain and I do not claim to.

What I can say is that those I speak with have told me their stories and shown me their triumphs. They have told me of their developed empowerment and capabilities that they could only have gained from meeting their challenges. This learning I have received from them has led me to the understanding that at least *eventually* it is worthwhile to look at every moment of our lives, no matter how painful, confusing, seemingly wrong or unjust, with complete gratitude. Whatever we face in life it will help us grow in some way. In some way gratitude will teach us, in some way we will realize that our life experience is a precious gift. The sooner we can achieve this gratitude, the sooner our pain will be relieved and our joy restored.

If you can immediately and continually look at *every moment* of your life in this way you will never feel yourself to be a victim. You will never feel less than anyone else, and you will literally never feel wronged or unloved. You will also never feel that God or the universe has abandoned you. If you can look at all of your life in this way you can find a state of complete inner peace and constant joy. If you want this joy, and if it is important enough to you to experience it, then you will make the *willful and conscious choice* to focus only on living in gratitude forever. You will make it one of your main life goals, and you will choose it as your single emotional focus and chosen emotional state and choose no other. If not, then you will focus on something else. You will focus on how unfair life is, how bad other people are, on how you were wronged, on how bad traffic is today or how bad the food at the local deli is or any of a million other discomforts of life and you will miss the miracle that all of life is. I hope and pray that you do not miss this opportunity that is available to you in every single moment of every day of your life.

Making this positive and powerful choice requires you to take charge of your life. It means choosing to become one hundred percent accountable for your emotional process at all times and to never again fall into the trap of blaming anyone else for what you choose to feel, or when, where, how or why you choose to feel it. This is not a process of controlling your emotions; it is a process of focusing on living in a single chosen emotional state of loving gratitude. Granted this is a very different way of life from the way most people have been taught or conditioned to live; still it is a wonderful beneficial option that is open to you now.

This may seem like preposterous talk, you may say or feel that it is impossible to make such a choice or to manage your emotional process from moment-to-moment and that life is far too complex and stressful to accomplish this. I assure you that it is not. Like all things in life gratitude is a choice and like every emotion you feel in a day, gratitude is a choice, not merely an emotional reaction that you are a slave to or are powerless to affect. I am not saying that gratitude is easily achieved; I am saying that it is simple. Many things in life are very difficult to achieve and quite simple, and all are a choice. In this process your conscious intention, your understanding and your will power are your greatest allies. I would also suggest that if you believe in God that God can help you tremendously to achieve this goal and that without God it is far more difficult. For if you are not grateful to God who are you grateful to and who can you pray to for help? Praying to be empowered to find gratitude in every moment, in every situation, no matter how seemingly challenging, negative, wrong or harmful is a great way to start. If you can find it within yourself to give up all of your pain to God in exchange for total gratitude, then God can help you reclaim your Joy!

Like any major change in life, changing to see all of life with gratitude can bring up our fear. Therefore, as stated earlier I suggest using the "I am my fear ..." method to release any fears that impede you in reaching your goal of being in constant gratitude. Some example statements that may help are,

"I am my fear:

- of living in fearless gratitude to God for every moment and experience of my life forever
- of failing at living my life in constant gratitude
- that it is not possible or that it is just too hard to live my life in constant gratitude
- that other people will take advantage of me if I focus on living my life in constant gratitude
- that other people will not understand or respect my choice to live in gratitude
- that living in gratitude is foolish and a waste of time
- that living in gratitude is not practical or realistic

When we are working to live in gratitude many daily situations may trigger us emotionally in negative ways, and we may feel judgmental toward people we meet or toward situations we experience. All of these emotional reactions make it difficult to live in constant gratitude, and it is easy to feel we are failing at living in gratitude. If you find yourself reacting to anyone, anything or any situation negatively or judgmentally (including yourself) I suggest that you first release the judgment or anger immediately. This monitoring and releasing of your negative emotions as they dynamically arise during your day-to-day activities can become a habit that eventually diminishes your tendency to have negative emotions at all. You can do this with statements of:

- I am my judgment of (add the name of the situation or the person)
- I am my anger or my irritation at (add the name of the person or the situation)
- I am my fear of (add the name of the person or the situation)
- I am my feeling that this situation is unfair, wrong, unjust or shouldn't be happening
- I am my feeling that this situation or relationship isn't the way I want it to be
- I am the stress, worry, pressure or anxiety that I am feeling
- I am the frantic feeling I am feeling
- I am my rage at (add the name of the situation or the person)
- I am my terror of (add the name of the situation or the person)
- I am my feeling that I am being overwhelmed by my situation
- I am the boredom I am feeling OR I am my boredom
- I am the disgust, distain or revulsion I am feeling toward ...
- I am the condescension that I am feeling toward ...
- I am my feeling that I "have to" make this situation be the way I want it to be or turn out the way I want it to (whenever we feel that something *has to be* any certain way or that we *have to* do anything we are *always motivated by fear*. The feelings of "have to" are always driven by trying to fix something that we fear we have done wrong or messed up or failed at in the past.)
- I am my judgment of (you add in the names, behavior or choices)
- I am my judgment of or anger at (you add in the names, words, emotions, behaviors or attitude)

All of the above statements can help you to release yourself from reactive emotional states *which are not* states of complete gratitude and usually have their roots in subconscious fear of some sort. You may find that there are many different "parts" of yourself that you were previously unaware of in this process of monitoring your reactions to others. You may only become aware of these parts of yourself as you begin monitoring yourself, and come to realize just how "ungrateful" parts of you can be in any given day, and in any given situation. You may find that you have many negative attitudes toward life and relationships that you were totally unaware of as you monitor your own tendency to judge others and life situations. You will only become aware of them when you compare and contrast them with the intentional and willfully chosen state of "complete and total conscious gratitude for God, and everything and everyone in every moment".

If you constantly release these emotional reactive tendencies, and constantly ask God for help in doing so, these emotional reactive tendencies will affect you less and less over time. It takes time and discipline to find and methodically work with each of these parts of yourself that are not yet resonant with gratitude, still it is completely worth it to do so. Doing anything else can only lead to unhappiness, conflict, fear, anger, negativity, judgmentalness or something less than joy and inner peace.

Once you are out of these negative emotional states you are free to then choose to create a more consistent positive emotional state for yourself in all areas of your life. Learning to manage your emotional state from moment-to-moment is crucial if you want to someday attain consistent inner peace and joy by living in constant gratitude. Inner peace is a gift you can give yourself and one that you truly deserve.

You can release yourself from negative emotional states with the release techniques outlined in this book. As previously stated there are many other methods and ways of releasing negative emotions and I suggest working with all of them. Your inner peace and happiness are my goal and hope. It will of course help to consistently pray and ask for help from God, and of course it helps to consciously willfully intend gratitude at all times. You can also apply *positive affirmations* in regard to your process of developing gratitude, for example.

"I am my feeling of complete loving gratitude in every part of my being for God, everyone, everything and every experience of my life, in every moment of my life, now and forever!"

What is necessary in the long run is that you attain *complete congruency and alignment* with gratitude, throughout all parts of yourself. This is necessary, because paradoxically, until you do so you will not want be able to fully manifest what you want in life. The reason this is true is because when you are in a state of gratitude *you always feel deserving,* therefore it is easy to manifest what you want. If you are feeling undeserving, for any reason, in any part of your system, you cannot be in a state of gratitude in that part of your system. Therefore that part of you is not congruent with manifesting what you truly consciously want in life. It is busy doing "something else", such as being angry, judging, fearing or expecting people to be something other than who they really are. This is a main reason why people cannot manifest their dreams and desires in life. They feel undeserving of doing so and they have not realized that if they simply choose to live in gratitude that this feeling of being undeserving can be "overwritten" by the feeling of total gratitude. If you are totally congruent in gratitude you will literally fear nothing because you are *totally focused on your feelings of gratitude*, meaning receiving good, happy results, not fearful painful results or losses. A useful prayer to create a completely congruent state of gratitude, and thus joy and inner peace in every moment of your life is the following:

"Please God help make every part of me, including mind, body, emotions and soul absolutely congruent in complete gratitude for you, and everyone and everything I have or will ever experience in every moment of my life, forever."

In the process of living in gratitude it is necessary to understand and accept that *you do have fear and all other negative emotions*. Do not deny it, accept the situation and begin to work to learn to focus on gratitude while you methodically and continually release your fears and all other negative emotions and all judgmentalness as they arise, day by day. In this way, you can eventually find inner peace, joy and *love for yourself and everyone else, all the time*. I know you have probably not yet experienced this feeling in your life, still you can! I have personally experienced this, I know it exists and that is why I am telling you about it, I would not waste your time otherwise. I would not waste my time and effort writing this book to you if I did not fully believe this to be true. So, every time you recognize that something negative has appeared on your "emotional radar", forgive yourself if you feel it is necessary, and do not judge yourself, because you are only human like all of us and you have not in any way failed. Then ask God to please help you to bring that part of yourself into total congruence and alignment with complete and absolute gratitude now and forever.

Until you look at all of life with gratitude you will not *believe and feel deeply* that you deserve to be loved and to receive total abundance of all kinds and to have it all fulfilled. You will also not feel that everyone else also deserves this just as much as you do. Meaning that if you have any part of yourself that feels undeserving, then it is still unwilling to receive and be loved and accepted. So that part of you won't allow yourself to receive and to feel loved by God or by anyone else completely. Even though you are already loved by God and always have been, these parts of yourself just haven't allowed themselves to feel it because they are not conscious enough to realize that they deserve it or they do not feel safe doing so. It is a "which came first the chicken or the egg type of situation". Which came first, total gratitude for everything and everyone or the letting go of the feelings of not being deserving of what we want to be in gratitude for? (i.e. The love of God, love of yourself, joy, fulfillment, freedom and total abundance of all kinds). This understanding needs to be fully grounded in all parts of your system, even the parts of yourself that feel or fear that this is just too difficult or impossible to achieve.

Some optional clearing statements that may help you achieve this state are:

"I am my fear that I do not deserve to live in constant gratitude for the rest of my life"

"I am my fear that it is not possible for me to completely live in gratitude forever in all areas of my life"

Chapter 13: The "Stadium Lights Method" of Clearing Negative Emotions:

This method is generally applicable to clearing any detrimental emotional state that you no longer want to feel. As long as you can feel the emotion in your body that you want to clear, and feel where you feel it in your body, you can apply this method. This method is simple and direct, and requires only that you are willing to feel and work with your emotions to a minimal degree. The steps of the process are:

1. Close your eyes and take a few slow deep breaths and get in touch with how your emotions and your body feel at the present moment.

2. Focus on feeling the feeling that you want to clear, wherever you feel it in most your body. If you feel it in several places, simply focus on where you feel it *most intensely*. If you do not feel the feeling now, remember when you last felt it strongly in the past and focus on that emotion where ever it resides in your body.

3. In your mind's eye visualize the emotion in some way. Whether you see it as a dark cloud, a swirling tornado, a rock, an abyss, a red blob or however it makes sense to you to perceive it.

4. Once you "see it" visualize a miniature version of yourself walking right into the core or middle of the visualized feeling. This may be a little uncomfortable initially, still it will help to quickly resolve the feeling if you will bring yourself to do so.

5. Once you are in the center of the feeling, begin looking around in all directions, up, down, left, right, front and back. Do a complete 360 degree evaluation of whatever you see from inside the emotional space. You may see many things, they may not make sense to you, or they may give you profound insights with deep meaning.

   Some people see many things, some people see only swirling clouds of negative energy or emotion, everyone is different and unique, there is no right or wrong to this process. Relax, you cannot fail or do this process the "wrong" way. In any case you will get better and better with practice and your results can become more and more powerful. Whatever you see or do not see simply acknowledge it and move onto the next step.

6. Next, see the emotion you have envisioned and you standing within it, surrounded by thousands of white lights, similar to the bright white lights you would see surrounding the top of a baseball stadium.

7. Begin looking at all of the lights through the transparent wall of the emotion one at a time, as fast as you can, in every direction, until the detrimental emotion dissolves around you completely. It can even help to see the lights spinning very fast around you as you are looking at them. The lights are not only in front of you and behind you; they are also above you and below you. Looking in all directions will help you process all aspects of the emotion fully until it is completely gone.

8. Once the emotion is completely processed out, return to your normal vantage point of conscious presence and review how you now feel about the previous emotion.

Ask yourself these questions. Is it now gone completely? Is there any residue in any part of your body? If there is any part of the emotion left, repeat the process from the beginning on that part of the emotion, in that part of your body. If there is nothing left of the emotion you began working with you can move onto another detrimental emotion you want to clear.

Chapter 14: The White Sphere Emotional Clearing Technique:

This technique is a guided meditation technique, and unlike the other techniques in this book is purely spiritual in nature. In this method it is important that you are in a relaxed, quiet and comfortable space for the duration of the process. It works even better if the lighting is soft or low.

Emotional Clearing Steps:

1. Close your eyes and take a few slow deep breaths, drawing the air in through your nose and exhaling out through your mouth
2. Visualize a small point of white light in your mind's eye that is located far in the distance
3. Watch as the point of soft white light gets closer and closer and gradually increases in size as it comes closer
4. As the point of light gets closer you realize it is the light of spirit and you begin to feel its loving warmth radiating toward you
5. The sphere of white light continues to move closer to you until it is very large and right in front of and above you
6. It is now very bright and still it is easy to look at and very warm and welcoming, and you can feel the energy of love pouring from it toward you, filling your system with the light that it radiates
7. If you feel comfortable doing so, allow the energy of the sphere of white light to draw out all of the pain and trauma you have experienced from your whole life. Feel the pain being drawn out of your body and into the white sphere, watch it go as it does, visualize this flow of painful energy leaving your body
8. Watch all of pain and trauma flow out of you and disappear into the white light completely and see that the white light sphere is totally unchanged by having received it, it may even have gotten brighter
9. Next ask that all the spaces in your system that have previously held pain or trauma be filled with a golden light from the sphere, and that you be filled with this light directly from God
10. Watch as the golden energy flows into you from the white light sphere and see it fill all the areas of your system that have previously held pain, trauma or heart ache
11. Once the process is complete, thank spirit for the healing you have received
12. Watch the sphere slowly recede into the distance until it has again become the tiny point of white light
13. Take a few more slow deep breaths, feel yourself grounded in your body, move your arms and legs a little and then open your eyes

It is important to feel how you feel after working through this process. Evaluate the changes that have happened in your system. You may wish to journal your results in order to keep track of your progress.

Chapter 15: Working With Sanskrit Mantras To Resolve Fear:

Sanskrit Mantras are a spiritual method of working with fear and other of life's problems that have been used for thousands of years in India, Tibet and other countries to transform consciousness and to attain spiritual enlightenment. One key step in the process of attaining enlightenment is to release one's fears in order to be able to focus totally and fearlessly on one's spiritual path.

There are a number of Sanskrit Mantras available that can help with managing one's fears. I am listing a few here that I have worked with and learned over the years. I have included the phonetic pronunciation along with them to help readers more easily learn to pronounce them. These mantras can be found on the internet in vocally recorded form on YouTube.com or from many other internet sources if you need audio support to your process.

For an extensive resource for Sanskrit Mantras and in depth information on how to use them I would suggest looking into the works of Thomas Ashley Farrand at SanskritMantra.com. In using mantras in general I would suggest that you recite them to yourself (you need not recite them aloud; you can recite them silently to yourself, although proper pronunciation even to yourself is important). It is important to recite them at least 108 times per day for optimal effect. Generally reciting mantras more than 108 times per day is better. You can determine by the results you get what the optimal number is for you and your current situation.

Mantra to feel protected, safe and secure and to manage social or relationship stress:

Om Dum Durgayei Namaha

Phonetic Pronunciation: Ohm Doom Dur-Guy-Yay Nah-Mah-Hah

Mantra to transmute the energy of fear of all kinds:

Shante Prashante Sarva Bhaya Upasha Mani Swaha

Phonetic Pronunciation: Shaan-Tee Pra-Shaan-Tee Sar-Vah By-Yah Oo-Pash-Ah Mah-Nee Swah-hah

Mantra to transmute the energy of anger of all kinds:

Shante Prashante Sarva Krodha Upasha Mani Swaha

Phonetic Pronunciation: Shaan-Tee Pra-Shaan-Tee Sar-Vah Krow-Dah Oo-Pash-Ah Mah-Nee Swah-hah

Mantra to transmute the energy and emotion of resentment that builds up in relationships:

Shante Prashante Sarva Upanaha Upasha Mani Swaha

Phonetic Pronunciation: Shaan-Tee Pra-Shaan-Tee Sar-Vah Ooh-Pan-Ah-Hah Oo-Pash-Ah Mah-Nee Swah-hah

Mantra to transmute the energy of hatred (whether your own hatred or that which you are receiving from others):

Shante Prahshante Sarva Dveshha Upasha Mani Swaha

Phonetic Pronunciation: Shaan-Tee Pra-Shaan-Tee Sar-Vah Di-Vesh-Ah Oo-Pash-Ah Mah-Nee Swah-hah

Like any method of transforming one's life, you get out what you put in when it comes to mantras. I have found that choosing to commit to working with mantras over a long period of time yields the best results. The longer you work with them, the greater the results and the stronger and more positive their energetic influence in your life.

There are many mantras available on the internet to help one sleep. Getting plenty of quality rest is a way to help better manage one's stress and fear. The internet address for some excellent sleep facilitating mantras is listed below. My clients have found them beneficial in reducing fear and anxiety that can arise at night while trying to sleep. One of the mantras is designed to liberate you from whatever detrimental influence is keeping you from finding inner peace, and with inner peace you can sleep well, and this is my suggested favorite for readers. The suggested manner of use of this mantra is simply to begin to recite it at bed time, while focusing only on the words of the mantra and allowing no other thoughts to creep into your mind. If you wake up again in the middle of the night, simply begin reciting the mantra again until you again fall asleep. The longer you practice the mantra over a period of nights, the better I have found the results and its effect to be. The mantras are available at the following web site link by in an article by Ramdesh Kaur, titled "3 Mantras to Help Insomnia":

spiritvoyage.com

(http://www.spiritvoyage.com/blog/index.php/3-mantras-to-help-insomnia/)

Many people who have trouble sleeping also fear not being able to sleep and fear not getting the rest that they need. In addition to saying mantras to help you sleep, I also suggest that you use the "I am my fear" practice to release any fears you may have of not being able to sleep. This technique can be helpful if you tend to wake up in the middle of the night and find that you cannot get back to sleep. For example you could try some of the following statements at night if you cannot sleep:

- I am my fear that I will not get enough sleep
- I am my fear that I cannot fall asleep
- I am my fear that my fear and stress will keep me awake
- I am my fear that I will be too tired to work tomorrow
- I am my fear I will have bad dreams or nightmares
- I am my fear that my worries or anxiety will keep me awake
- I am my fear that my constantly running thoughts will keep me awake

Once our fears and worries are released, including those related to sleep itself we tend to find it much easier to fall into a restful sleep.

Chapter 16: Many of Us Live Our Lives As Victims, Perpetrators and Rescuers:

Our world, in many people's views, is made up of innocent victims of wrongdoing and guilty perpetrators of those perceived wrongs. In other words *the good people and the bad people*. In addition there is another group which are not spoken of quite as often whom we could call rescuers. Rescuers are sometimes seen as a group of selfless good people who help the victims and may also be seen to work to stop the wrong doers. Those of us who hold to these simple views of the world, life and relationships are not fully aware of the limiting implications of holding these beliefs about the world as a whole. Nor are we aware of their detrimental effects on humanity's development and evolution and processes of learning from our experiences and interactions with others. The dualistic belief that there are victims automatically assumes that there must be perpetrators and vice versa. If there are victims there must be someone to rescue them. This approach to life is in its essence incredibly limiting, polarizing, blinding and misleading. This distorted set of projections onto our reality creates confusion, conflict, misunderstanding, pain and a tendency to judge ourselves and each other constantly. I am not suggesting that good and evil do not exist in the world; I am only suggesting that these particular ways of attempting to categorize life are too simplistic and thus detrimental. I will explain in the paragraphs below what I mean by these statements.

A great deal of work has been developed on the victim/perpetrator/rescuer model (V/P/R model) of human interaction in the past. The information in this book is based upon personal practice with clients rather than research into existing articles on this topic. It is important to give credit to the developer of the original model, (see the original 1968 article on the "Drama Triangle" by Stephen Karpman, M.D. entitled: "Fairy Tales and Script Drama Analysis" http://www.karpmandramatriangle.com/pdf/DramaTriangle.pdf). In this article the three basic roles of victim, *persecutor* and rescuer are described. Since that time many derivative works and further deeper analysis have been developed and are of course well worth studying.

The descriptions of the roles in the following paragraphs are meant to explain the basics of an emotional and mental process and mindset that starts with "victimhood", as well as the victim/perpetrator/rescuer model overall. These descriptions are also meant to define the relationship between victimhood and our core fears, our desire for safety and control, and how we use our judgmentalness and punishment of self and others to *try* to achieve safety. Safety is seen here not always as actual physical safety, often it is simply the feeling of being safe or being "safer" than we would otherwise be if we did not function within the role of victim or rescuer, etc.. These descriptions are also designed to show how judgmentalness of self and others is the key support mechanism to the victim/perpetrator/rescuer model and system of dynamics.

In this discussion I am not judging any of the V/P/R roles as bad or saying that anyone is wrong to operate from any of them. Humans could not do without these roles in our current level of social and emotional development and evolution as a species. We have not yet learned how to unconditionally love and accept one another and how to immediately forgive each other for anything and everything, which is the most optimal mode of interpersonal function. We *have* previously needed a simple set of "rules of the road" for interpreting reality, social situations and interpersonal dynamics to support our decision-making. These roles have previously been a key part of our process of social learning as individuals and a core element of the process of our species learning to evolve its social systems. However life and the world have both lately and rapidly become too complex for these simple roles to be applicable, and we have now out grown their usefulness. Therefore they have become an encumbrance for us as individuals and as a species. We cannot continue functioning from the vantage point of the victim/perpetrator/rescuer model if we want to continue to have a functioning society in the future and good quality relationships. Our relationships are too complex, our society is too complex, our technology is too complex, our world is too complex, our problems are too complex and change is happening far too rapidly for such simplistic interpretive mechanisms to be constructive applied to our lives. We need new ways of attaining *conscious discernment* and operating from vantage points of discerning decision-making which do not involve being judgmental and which are not fear based. We must become willing to change, to learn and to grow and to adopt new and more sophisticated ways of interpreting ourselves, our interactions with others and the larger world. This means being willing to reevaluate ourselves, our mental functions, emotional functions and decision-making functions at every level of granularity and in every area of life and relationship. Until we are willing to throw away these old worn out social and interpersonal roles and methods we will not be willing to design and utilize new ones. If we attempt to build our world's future social systems and systems of interpersonal relationship dynamics upon a foundation of these distorted misunderstandings of ourselves and each other, and the very poor values of fear, judgmentalness and the V/P/R roles we can only create more problems than solutions.

The V/P/R model creates many dysfunctional and maladaptive social and interpersonal dynamics which may appear on the surface to have benefit. However in reality these roles, especially that of victim, tend to poison our relationships and our emotional process. I am not in any way denigrating those who have gone through war, or who have experienced personal trauma or abuse of any kind. I am especially not diminishing the experience of women or children who have experienced trauma or abuse of various kinds, including sexual abuse. In this discussion if we are speaking of victims then we are speaking of a person who is living in or who has bought into a "victim mindset", not simply a person who has experienced abuse or trauma. There is a significant difference.

Any of us, after experiencing a trauma could for a time feel ourselves to be a victim; almost no one is immune to this type of experiential interpretation. It could be said that it is even *necessary* for us to go through this disempowered state or feeling for a period of time in order to heal or to eventually make full sense of the experience of trauma. We may have no other way of coping with the experience and this initial interpretation is simply one step on the path to eventual healing. I am not judging the mindset or saying that it is wrong to be in it. I am saying that we can learn not to fall into it in the first place and train our children not to, if we choose to. I am saying that there are more advantageous interpretations of difficult or even traumatic life experience that we can make than victimhood. If we make this choice to learn a different way to interpret difficult situations we can change our lives and the world for the better. This is simply an optimal choice. Victimhood and feeling victimized is not wrong or bad, it is simply a choice that we can make. We all have the opportunity, with enough information and attained understanding to make better choices.

My intention in this writing is ultimately to *reduce human suffering* by helping people transcend the whole process of interpreting themselves or others in the limiting and disempowering roles of victims, perpetrators or rescuers. An additional intention of this writing is to help people learn that judging each other for any reason is ultimately a detrimental process of control seeking that is doomed to failure, and that here there are also better alternatives.

Trauma and abuse of all kinds are real and terrible and their affects are also real, and often last a lifetime. The wars, genocides and acts of slavery of our world are real and have happened. How we choose to emotionally deal with past and present difficult events and experiences, as we gradually heal over the course of our lives, is up to each of us. Learning to reinterpret our painful experiences and *our perceived roles* in those experiences is a key to learning to heal from our past experiences and regain our personal power. In effect we become empowered when we learn how to *change how we remember and interpret our past* and thus to change it and grow from it. When we change how the past happened to us in our memory we then literally change the pain that we hold in relation to it. We also potentially change how powerful we feel in relation to our past experiences and thus how powerful we feel in the present moment. This process is not mere "mind games", it is real, meaningful and is powerful and brings with it true insight and deep understanding of ourselves, our relationships, the world and our lives.

In my view the labels of victim, perpetrator and rescuer that we apply to ourselves and others are in the long term detrimental to our process of healing and learning from life experience in general. They keep us from forgiving ourselves and others, and of letting go of our limiting expectations of self and others, and by doing so freeing ourselves to move on from the past. They can leave us feeling disempowered and believing that life is unfair, as in situations where we have given up our lives and health for our families, or those we love, in our attempt to "rescue" them and keep them safe.

In simple terms we may in past situations have seen ourselves in the positive role of a rescuer and have seen others in the negative role as perpetrators. We may have even looked at detrimental *situations* as the "perpetrators" we are saving those we love from, as in mothers or fathers working endlessly to make ends meet to support their families. In these situations parents can feel that painful and limiting situations they feel trapped in are the perpetrators of their lives that they feel victimized by. This can be so when we are trapped in conditions of poverty or where there are no available jobs, while we are trying to support a family.

In some cases it can happen that in the end, after having given all we can to protect and support those we love, that we are left with nothing, and thus we then feel victimized and empty, and without perceived solution to our detrimental feelings. This can happen in cases of divorce after many years of having tried to make a relationship work for the sake of our children. It can also happen in situations of caretaking those we love who are sick for long periods of time, only to have them die, leaving us feeling lost, grieving and abandoned. In these situations life can seem totally unfair and wrong, and we can feel lost and alone in our fear of the perceived wrongness of it all. Trying to make sense of life from the victim/perpetrator/rescuer model of life is too simple a process to apply to the far more complex social and emotional world we actually live in. When we try to use this model we become limited, stuck, confused, dejected, depressed, angry and resentful. We also tend to judge ourselves and others and get stuck in negative emotional dynamics without seeing any positive ways to achieve resolution, aside from playing "either the victim or the rescuer" again.

Using the V/P/R labels and roles disempowers us. Using these labels and their associated roles ends up creating more fear, pain and misunderstanding, and limits our ability to constructively process our past pain and trauma. Using these roles requires us to *hold onto our pain,* rather than leaving it behind, so that we can then heal and move forward with our lives and emotionally live in the present. When we interpret life from any of the three roles of the V/P/R model we are *trying to empower* ourselves, *disempower* others and *control* life situations by applying the victim/perpetrator/rescuer process. Not realizing that it will in the end take us nowhere, and that in effect it is a "skipping record dynamic" that goes on and on.

We want to see ourselves as good; we want to see perpetrators or perpetrator situations as "bad" so that we can rationalize working against perpetrators without guilt, shame, emotional conflict or remorse. This is how we get over our internal conflict; an extreme example of this is found in war and in even in other kinds of battle, such as business, politics and divorces. This is why it is so important for us to harshly judge and even "demonize" the enemy when we go to and fight a war, rather than to see the enemy's humanity. How else could one bring oneself to kill another person without hesitation and without reacting with deep feelings of guilt, shame and remorse?

Sometimes we find ourselves in the perpetrator role, convinced that we have the right to harshly affect or even punish others because we have previously been wronged. Sometimes we feel we have to rescue a perceived victim from someone who is unfairly abusing them, and in the process we risk our own security. If we lose our security because of having risked it to save someone else we may then feel victimized ourselves. Where does the cyclic process end?

The V/P/R process is neither real nor true, it is only something we project onto relationships and situations; it is however believed in and emotionally bought into by many people, especially when we feel that life has not been fair to us or those we love. Perceived unfairness and other forms of comparison, as well as our own pain and fear, are our key rationalizations for applying the V/P/R model in a judgmental way.

The V/P/R model is, at its foundation, driven by fear and is based upon and driven by a judgmental mindset. The basic desire of this judgmental mindset is to achieve control and thereby to achieve safety, although it never really does achieve this goal. Meaning that we want to *feel* we are in control of our lives, ourselves and others, even though we cannot be. Therefore we judge ourselves, and our lives and we judge others constantly, and continue to do so, as we fail to achieve our goals of attaining control. We continue doing it, despite the havoc it creates in our lives and in the world. In effect we are saying that if I just believe enough in the V/P/R model then I can supposedly control my life, control others and thus will be safe. It is a form of denial of reality and the results of our actions and decisions in order to achieve a false *feeling* of safety.

In our day-to-day life, though we rarely realize it, most of us shift and cycle through the three roles, moving from victim to perpetrator to rescuer and back again, throughout the day. Continually rationalizing and justifying when, where, how and why it is necessary for *us* to do so, and why others are either right or wrong for being in the particular V/P/R roles they choose to be in. As stated earlier these dynamics are all driven by the process of fear driven judgmentalness. The process of judgmentalness is driven by the simple desire to control ourselves and other's choices, emotions, thoughts, behaviors and situational results.

What I am illustrating in this section is that although we can inadvertently become lost in any of the three roles for extended periods of time, the victim mindset is often the start of, and the root of, the whole three part dynamic and problem. The victim mindset can even become a *way of life* for some of us without our realizing it has happened. In this way we rationalize disempowering ourselves and rationalize not taking constructive empowered decisive action in our lives or in our self-healing process on a consistent basis. The other two roles, (rescuer and perpetrator) can also become lifestyles; however they could be considered more empowered states, although in a maladaptive way. All three roles actually have the potential to rationalize taking punitive action against someone. (i.e. The victim may take righteous vengeance on the perpetrator. The perpetrator may harm the victim, often motivated by their own fear and pain. The rescuer is often societally supported or allowed to punish the perpetrator in order to rescue the victim.) None of the three roles is suggested as either a lifestyle choice or as a useful role at any time. In the end all three roles are driven at their foundation by the emotion of fear.

To perceive and *fully identify* oneself as a victim can be to embrace, consciously or subconsciously, many other erroneous and disempowering beliefs about life, oneself and about perceived perpetrators, for example:

Some people who are heavily identified with the victim mindset feel themselves to be *completely innocent,* and feel that they have been wounded or wronged, and therefore may see themselves to have *no responsibility* for their situation or their woundedness or abuse. Whereas the perceived perpetrator or wrong doer is often seen by them as *fully responsible*, as not innocent, and any harm that may have been done *to the perpetrator* in the situation has less meaning or no real meaning at all. This occurs because the situation and its results were supposedly the perpetrator's fault to begin with. This is a polarized and unbalanced interpretation of events, power dynamics, relationships and situations, which ultimately inhibits resolution and self-healing, and keeps old fear, pain and trauma in place. These interpretations also undermine the potential for achieving forgiveness of the perpetrator, social or relationship healing, reconciliation, and even negotiation for compensation for the pain caused to humans by other humans. If we cannot at some point take some appropriate responsibility for managing our woundedness how can we ultimately take responsibility for our process of self-healing? These statements are not designed to "blame the victim". They are only designed to suggest that at some point in our healing process it helps us to make the shift into a state of empowered consciousness for our own benefit.

The perpetrator may be perceived to be the *sole cause* of the negatively perceived situation. If so then the person who defines themselves as the victim may feel entitled to compensation of some sort for the perceived problem or wrong doing. In addition, the victim may feel that the perpetrator(s) deserve punishment and/or to supply the compensation. I am not suggesting that people who have been abused or traumatized do not deserve reparation. I am simply suggesting that if those who have been abused can *only* see the situation from a polarized vantage point then their view cannot be *completely balanced or accurate*. Therefore they cannot optimize their views *for their own highest interest or that of society*. Meaning that if the information that they are using to interpret their situation is not *completely accurate*, it is not optimally useful in helping them heal themselves and learn from their life experiences. This could be true whether we are speaking of victims of abuse or *perpetrators of abuse* who have, due to having experienced prior abusive situations themselves, turned to expressing themselves in abusive ways.

People who feel victimized *may be* so focused on their pain and their judgments of the perpetrator that they feel no responsibility to change themselves or their emotional process. In these situations they become unable to change their behaviors, their emotional processes, their mindsets, their situational interpretations or beliefs in regard to their feelings of woundedness, or how the situation of perceived abuse occurred. This interpretation is not facilitative of constructive, positive and proactive self-healing as it does not require a person who feels themselves to have been victimized to learn anything empowering or constructive from their experiences. In this situation I am simply suggesting that if we can at some point in our healing process choose to learn whatever we can from it, we will then be empowered by it to some degree, and made stronger by doing so. Again I am suggesting that all life experiences, as terrible as they can be, can also be sources of strength and empowerment and of greater understanding and wisdom.

In *victim / perpetrator / rescuer think* there must always someone at fault, to be blamed and / or to be punished. This statement applies to the mindset of all three roles. Meaning that nothing ever just "happens" in the world of V/P/R and everything that happens is attributed to the states or processes of victimhood/perpetration and rescuing. Therefore we can't just move on with life after a traumatic or devastating occurrence, because there is *always the fear of further victimization or the potential for need for rescue.* In addition the perceived requirement of blame and punishment dynamics must supposedly be met *before we can move on;* this dynamic tends to create more perpetrators as righteous victims become vengeful perpetrators. Therefore we become stuck in in the V/P/R process, rather than rapidly releasing fear and pain of the past and *forgiving,* and thereby healing ourselves, and leaving the past behind and living in the present. Many people in spousal relationships become stuck in a repetitive judgmental cycle of bitter criticism. This leads to ongoing poisonous animosity and resentment, and this then becomes a cycle of inability to forgive and move on. This *choice to hold onto fear, judgmentalness, pain and resentment* undermines their capacity to create joy in their own lives and deprives them of future relationship happiness.

Situations of perceived abuse are in some way inherently interpreted to be *unfair* to the victim mindset or in principle *wrong.* If we choose to interpret and label situations in black and white terms as "either right or wrong and fair or unfair" and ourselves as the victim of such dynamics we are again stuck. This occurs when we fear we could supposedly *again become the victim* of such dynamics, or when we feel we are still "owed something" by the perpetrator, or the world, for our pain. Life is not black and white, it is neither fair nor unfair, neither right nor wrong. Again we must first release the fear (even if it is just the fear of missing out on the "just rewards of our perceived victimhood"), before we feel safe moving forward in life. Victims can receive many rewards for being victims, (i.e. attention, energy, public focus, money, support, less expectation by others of being self-responsible, not being required to deal directly with their unresolved pain, etc.) Who in their "right mind" would want to give up this preferred status in our tremendously difficult and demanding world? Consciously recognizing and disengaging from these dynamics is essential if we want to quickly heal ourselves, center ourselves in our own sovereign power and move on with our lives.

When we feel victimized we tend to inherently see ourselves as *good,* and the perpetrator is usually inherently and unquestionably seen as *bad or wrong.* This too is a very black and white interpretation; life has far more gray areas than this interpretation tends to reveal. Victims often feel they have the right to blame perpetrators and even the duty to do so, if only because "they are the victim". We can fear letting the perpetrators off "scot-free" and moving on with our lives. Doing so can feel unjust or even wrong as if by doing so that we ourselves would in some way become perpetrators. We can even fear our own guilt, shame or self-judgment or the judgment of others for doing so. If we cannot release these fears we are again stuck in the past, due to unresolved fear without realizing it.

There are people today who feel they have been victimized by other individuals. They may then *also* feel victimized by either the lack of support or of the *expectations* of their families. They could also feel victimized in this same way by their chosen social groups, the companies they work for, their governments, the world in general, or even in their relationships with their chosen religion. It is often not an option to find justice or the support that we need for our self-healing process in the world around us. Therefore it is necessary to learn to self-reliantly release our past pain through some independent process that we manage for ourselves, so that we can at least find self-empowered inner peace for our own sake. That is in part what this book is about.

"Perpetrators deserve punishment and to be *controlled* so that they cannot hurt us or others again, and victims cannot be safe unless perpetrators are controlled and punished". In this situation we fear not being in control of perpetrators. Of course *complete control* of anyone is an illusion and cannot happen, although we all do have some degree of *power and influence*. Our fear wants us to try to be "in complete control".

Therefore we often become stuck in trying repeatedly to affect control over perceived perpetrators in order to bring them "completely into line with our expectations" so that we can feel safe.

Some people call their personal expectations "justice" whereas others see that this is just a rationalization for control driven by fear or an expression of their personal preferences on the world. I am not suggesting letting oneself be abused. I am suggesting using your personal power and influence to assure that you are as safe and emotionally whole as you *practically and realistically* can be. If you come from fear you will try to control unrealistically. If you give up your fear you will apply all your power and influence wisely and consciously and in a balanced manner, and will not waste your time or energy with fear. You cannot optimize your application of your power until you give up your fear because you will always try too hard, and you will always try to control, rather than to wisely influence the world in a balanced manner. Fear is in effect an inefficient and ineffective waste of time and energy, which can be better spent elsewhere.

This attempted control dynamic is often seen in marriage relationships as well as in parental relationships when we try to attain our expectations or specific desired results due to subconscious fear. We can become consumed in the unbalanced process of trying to control the behavior of those we "love", either out of fear for them, or fear of the results of their choices or fear of their abandonment. Fear driven decisions are not decisions driven by love, it is important to discern the difference. Whatever the reasons for our fears, if we do not first release our fear of *not being in control* of the other person, then we will continue to try to control them. This means we will continue to be in conflict with them that is *irreconcilable*, because people simply do not want to be controlled and all of us have free-will. For many people the closest they have ever come to loving someone else is trying to control them.

We try to control our children to keep them safe and to keep ourselves safe from their potentially unwise decisions. Not even very young children can be completely controlled, as any experienced parent will tell you. It is a paradox that the people we love the most are often the ones we feel most motivated to control, to our detriment as well as theirs. The only solution to this ongoing conflict of interests is to first release our subconscious fears and then to develop conscious ways to positively negotiate with those we are in relationship with from a place of fearless peaceful and loving conscious understanding.

When we feel we have been victimized we may feel that we have been sensitive, feeling and functioning in a *socially acceptable and humane manner* and that the perpetrator is not or has not. We may see anyone we love that is resisting our control as a perpetrator by the way, and we may fully rationalize our judgmentalness and criticisms of them as just or "justice". If we hold this perspective our fear is filtering our interpretations and we are not able to empathize with the other person's situation and motivations. If this is the case then we are not making decisions based upon the *whole reality of the situation* and will be unable to clearly see anyone else's point of view. So we will make decisions that are unwise and uninformed and which are neither discerning nor insightful. These kinds of decisions can only result in conflict, problems, misunderstandings, miscommunications and repeatedly unresolved disputes. This is not a recipe for peaceful relationship negotiation.

Demonization of perpetrators can feel good and empowering in the moment and can help us feel better about ourselves, yet it does not help us heal ourselves or relationships, or help us move on from emotional trauma. In reality the V/P/R model is only an ego self-defense mechanism human beings have created to try to understand and control social situations and relationships and we can dispense with it completely. In order to do so we must give up our fear, our illusions of safety, our willingness to judge ourselves and each other and choose not to participate in the V/P/R roles to any degree.

When we feel victimized we tend to feel powerless and to feel that perpetrators are more powerful than we are. This misinterpretation leads to a misperception of our own power, and creates a significant re-triggering of our fear when we look back upon the situation. When our fear is re-triggered we feel disempowered in making decisions in the present. It also limits our feelings of empowerment when we envision our future. The interpretation of victimhood is to a degree a false and covert process of *trying to empower ourselves* by feeling good about ourselves. (i.e. Seeing ourselves as innocent, powerless, right, just and worthy of the support of others as well as entitled to the support of others in our process of seeking retribution or compensation). It is necessary to realize this *potentially* dark side of victimhood, as it can be seductive. It can also become a subconscious motivation to hold onto the role of victim, which is ultimately a disempowered state and a distorted point from which to interpret relationships and reality.

Again the solution is to first release the fear we feel, through whatever means you choose, and then to see the truth of the situation more clearly for what it is. The truth is that we always have some degree of power and the capacity to influence our relationships at every moment of our lives, as well as some *participation* in any relationship problem or conflict that exists. It is important that you fully realize your personal power, and through doing so find greater peace and joy in your life and relationships. We never completely lose our power of choice, and all of the roles in the V/P/R model are only based upon an illusion that we project onto life and our relationships.

Certainly our choices can be *extremely diminished* in many life situations and relationships, and when we are afraid our perspective can make our free-will appear to be non-existent. That is how fear affects our consciousness, it is blinding and diminishing and leads us to falsely perceive ourselves as weak and powerless, even if that is not truly the case at all. Fear creates a sort of limiting tunnel vision effect on life and our choices. Some life situations can be so dire as to push us to the point where it may appear that the only choice left to us is how we choose to interpret what is happening in the moment, and how we choose to feel about it. Still this small choice is a choice that no one can take away from us.

Many people may at this point speak of situations of child abuse and ask what power of choice do children have? I would respond and say that at the time of their abuse they had *very little* if any awareness, understanding or choice at all. This is so in part because of their lack of conscious awareness and knowledge, and in part their ignorance due to their youth and lack of development and in part due to society's ignorance of the terrible pervasiveness of child abuse and lack of adequate preventative support to these abused children. I would *then say* that from the point in their lives after they have been abused and begun to grow up that their power of choice *increases* and that they often begin to have more and more ability to change their lives for the better and to learn from their past. I base this perspective upon years of working with many adults who were the victims of early life child abuse. They, like all of us, will likely at some point in their lives have the ability to change their emotional history by releasing their negative trapped emotions and thereby free themselves from their past. Over the years I have seen the immense courage that it takes for these people to transcend their past experiences and face their fears. I have both watched and helped them do so. I have facilitated them in conquering their fears and seen them become far more powerful in the process by realizing the strength they truly have. In the process of their self-healing they tend to leave behind their illusions of their own powerlessness and embrace their power to create their own lives. Some of them are the strongest and most loving people I know. A big part of the healing process for these people is learning to re-interpret their early life experiences in a more conscious, astute, mature, knowledgeable way.

Everyone has the choice to determine their emotional process and to manage it from moment-to-moment, though we may not have previously realized this. We only need the tools and in some cases support and facilitation in learning to do so. Many people believe that others "make them feel" what they feel or that they have no choice as to how they feel about anything in life. They may also believe that they cannot change how they felt in the past about what they experienced, and I assure you that this is not true at all. If you learn to release your fears with the methods included in this book, or through other methods, which are available from many other sources, you can prove this belief untrue. You can prove that you are the determiner of whether you fear or do not fear. If you determine whether or not you *choose to fear*, no one can ever fully control your choices or your life experience. If you choose to give up this power to determine how you feel, then you will be choosing to live in a process of only reacting to what happens around you. I would suggest that this is not all that life can be and that you deserve much better.

Some people who feel victimized feel that if others "knew" the perpetrator as they do, that they would or should probably judge them and feel as negatively about them as the victim does. "If others do not agree with me it is probably because they do not understand the situation and my experience as I do". It is simply a fact that there are many damaged, dangerous and even terribly dysfunctional people in this world who do cause great harm, and who do abuse others. (i.e. Perpetrators, who themselves are often prior victims of abuse for example). In spite of this fact, if we want to heal ourselves and create better lives, it is crucial for us to learn to focus on some other way of interpreting life and relationships that is more empowering and positive. We must release our fear and pain that has kept us imprisoned by keeping us focused on the negative, on our perceived limitations, on limited interpretations of others, and on the past.

We can shift our conscious focus onto the loving, kind aspects of life and loving people in the world and even choose to see the pure soul given to each of us by God in those who have harmed us. When we make this conscious choice to do so, we can find it within ourselves to forgive, to heal the past and to move on. The phrase, "there but for the grace of God go I" may help in this regard. I am not suggesting living a

"Pollyanna" type of life and ignoring the negative aspects of life or hiding from abusive people. I am not suggesting being impractical or being unwilling to defend oneself when and where appropriate. I am suggesting that fearing anything in life is a dysfunctional, maladaptive and ineffective way of dealing with it. I am also suggesting that managing your focus of consciousness in an empowered positive way helps one become capable of attaining a consistent level of inner peace while remaining effectively able to achieve one's life goals.

Due to their focus on their unresolved pain or trauma some people who feel victimized feel unable to see the part their own decisions and ways of making decisions may have played in the abuse or trauma they have endured. Others tend to see the opposite view of the situation as if everything they endured was "all their fault" and blame everything on themselves. They may also arrive at a conclusion that they *only make mistakes* or that they just don't know how to make good decisions at all. Both kinds of interpretations are unbalanced and therefore inaccurate. Neither is optimally supportive or constructive in regard to self-healing, because both views are judgmental in nature and focused on finding fault with self or a fault with a perpetrator in the situation. Judgmentalness in any form is not supportive of healing.

Focusing only on a perpetrator's actions to the exclusion of our own actions disempowers us in our process of learning from our experiences. Focusing only on our own actions does the same thing. It is best for us to become willing at some point to look deeply and discerningly at what part we and our decision-making processes, behaviors, thoughts, ways of interpreting situations, beliefs and emotions have played in the results of the past. Then we can become willing to learn from them and to change any or all of these for the better. Again I do not believe in blaming victims of abuse for their situations and this set of statements is not designed to do so. I do not believe in blame at all as a constructive process of dealing with social or emotional situations or ills. I also do not believe in blaming perpetrators or rescuers as this is simply a process of judgment and is also a waste of time. I do believe in teaching everyone how to transcend all of these detrimental dynamics. My statements are meant to optimally empower victims of abuse, *as well as to help perpetrators in need of healing so that they will no longer abuse others, and to help rescuers cease to mindlessly rescue victims and judgmentally punish perpetrators.* I am interested in *informing rescuers* who tend to inadvertently harm themselves by giving of themselves in an unbalanced manner in hopes of being redeemed, avoiding abandonment or avoiding some other subconscious fear they do not even realize they have.

Another vantage point to look at the mindsets and roles of victimhood and rescuing from is that both can be a method of seeking to find an external solution to an internal emotional state. Of course perpetrators are also doing the same thing. Victims may seek external punishment for perpetrators in order to find closure. Rescuers may seek recognition, self-worth, self-esteem or some form of self-justification via their rescuing efforts. I am not denigrating the efforts of those who lovingly give of themselves to protect or serve others. What I am seeking to illuminate is that some of us are in some part of ourselves subconsciously holding detrimental emotional issues or extremely negative feelings about ourselves that can only be resolved through internal work, and that it is vital to understand that this is the case. If we are emotionally wounded and do not realize it we may seek to sooth our wounds through external means without understanding that this is the strategy of managing our own pain that we are employing. These strategies are generally not very effective and in a way are an addiction, meant to distract us from our own underlying and unresolved pain or woundedness. The flip side of the situation is that for a time the V/P/R roles can be seen as a helpful buffer of sorts in that they keep us unaware of underlying pain we are not yet ready to deal with. In essence we may need to become stronger and to learn more about ourselves before we feel that we are ready to tackle our internal problems or wounds. This can be especially necessary if we do not have adequate healing support from our family, medical system or our society to help us with our problematic life issues.

We can spend a lifetime rescuing others and giving of ourselves without really getting to a point of self-acceptance, self-forgiveness, healing feelings of shame or guilt, attaining authentic feelings of self-worth or attaining comprehensive feelings of unconditional self-love. These positive and conscious internal emotional and mental states can only be fully arrived at *in a lasting way* through *internal work* and attainments of *self-awareness*. The V/P/R roles can sometimes give us emotional boosts and support along the way and help us to see ourselves in a better light. This process can be a stepping stone to our being willing to then go deeper in our internal self-forgiveness work and self-love development work. However they are not a substitute for it and they cannot directly lead to these states.

Unfortunately society has not developed to the point where it teaches this type of self-developmental and self-healing process to all world citizens in a standardized manner. Therefore people go through the same process of learning NOT to function fearfully and judgmentally, in the V/P/R roles, by going through the experiential school of hard knocks. We can as a species no longer afford this degree of evolutionary inefficiency and ineffectiveness in our process of social and individual development. As people become more *empowered technologically*, and world population pressures increase, there is now too much potential for people to act out in detrimental ways, as terrorists do. Therefore we need to quickly teach people not to function this way any longer on a global scale. It is because of this evolving situation and growing social and technological dynamic that fear is the most dangerous force in our world. In our current world situation the V/P/R model has become the *perfect and endless justification and excuse* for terrorists to terrorize, for governments to wage war, for police to abuse criminals, for abusers to abuse victims, and for victims to seek vengeance on abusers. It is also a built in excuse for the global system and individuals *not to significantly learn* from their own past ignorant series of unwise decisions. It is a cycle that the world has become stuck in, to its detriment. Where does it all end? How does the situation get better if we do not change the fundamental emotional dynamics and decision-making strategies that are creating the situation at every level of relationship and society?

I would say that whatever has happened in our lives can be learned from, and can thus empower us to change for the better. I suggest that victims, perpetrators and rescuers can all learn from the review their prior experiences, and from the vantage point of each role. If you choose to do so you will learn something worthwhile. Even if the learning appears to be small or inconsequential in the moment it can pay off in big ways in the future. In this way we may learn to keep whatever negative experiences that have occurred in the past from happening again. At the very least we may simply better inform some other area of our lives, our minds or our emotional processes through our experiential learning.

Some people who feel victimized feel they have no responsibility for management of their *personal power* or free-will choices in their situation of victimhood or abuse. We all have free-will at all times and if we choose to be accountable for the application of our personal power and our choices at all times then we are more likely to remain conscious and thus able to make wise decisions. This is the essence of learning to be more discerning. Choosing to be self-accountable does not mean we "made our victimhood or abuse happen". It means that we can choose to be self-accountable for digging ourselves out of our perceived situation of victimhood as soon as we possibly can, and to re-empower ourselves sooner, whenever we are emotionally ready to do so.

Some people who feel victimized feel it is necessary to judge and even hate perpetrators for their perceived actions without feeling guilty for their judgmentalness and with assumed social and emotional impunity. I would say that although the victim/perpetrator/rescuer model is heavily bought into by society at all levels, it does not mean that this model and its implications are actually good for us as individuals or as a society. Even if hating appears to be for a "good or necessary reason" such as in fighting the war on terrorism. Holding onto hatred poisons us, even while we are hoping that it will poison those we hate.

Attacking and punishing hatred for hatred sake shows a poor understanding of hatred in general and what its roots are and it shows a lack of willingness on the part of society to deal with what creates the fundamental emotional states of hatred in the first place. It is our own indifference to the needs of our own citizenry that initially breeds hatred. It is far better to preemptively and proactively deal with the roots of fear. We need to heal fear and hatred in our society by investing in the people who are stressed, disempowered, disenfranchised, and afraid. Rather than by punishing hatred after the fact of our indifference to each other's developmental needs, when it comes out as social expressions of fear driven resentment, hatred and violence.

Sometimes people who feel victimized believe or rationalize that since they have been abused that they have the right to be insensitive to or even to abuse others. They may even abuse others who were not involved in their original wounding, without guilt and with assumed impunity, due to their wounded or impaired status. This can occur when the victims of child abuse in turn *sometimes* become abusers of their own children. We might refer to these prior victims as perpetrators. Violence is never the solution to any problem; it is almost always the source of problems.

Wounded people may bully others in order to feel safe from potentially being abused by others and in order to prove to themselves that they are safe from potential perpetrators. They may also act to preemptively criticize attack or intimidate others to keep those others from judging, abandoning or punishing them. They may even feel it is okay to actually openly seek revenge on those they perceived harmed them, (again without guilt, remorse or responsibility). In these cases the perceived victim becomes an active "perpetrator" without realizing it. Oddly enough many of what we might see as the worst perpetrators are simply people who have, at a subconscious level, rationalized their most negative behaviors through interpreting themselves as victims of past events or relationships. The *freedom of their perpetration* is part of the "reward" they feel they are owed for their victimhood.

I perceive much of the dynamic of the bullying problems that are being seen in schools these days to be the acting out of emotionally fearful or wounded children who see themselves as victims rationalizing their bullying, (i.e. perpetration). Oddly enough in my work I have even seen teachers bullying children, due to fear of the children "attacking or embarrassing" them; this is just how conflicted and misunderstood the situation has become.

Some people who feel victimized feel they have the right to demand punishment of the perpetrator from those who love them, from society at large, or via the judicial system. Some of us cannot let go of the past and our focus on our pain until we feel that others have *literally* experienced our pain. This tendency keeps us from healing ourselves and moving on. This dynamic is also driven by the fear of not having the power to affect those whom we have been profoundly negatively affected or hurt by. This fear, like all fears, can be released. This process of wanting others to feel our pain can be seen merely as revenge seeking, or it can be seen as necessary for the victim to prove to themselves they do have personal power. However in some cases I also see it as a way for the victim to try to feel safe and sure that others really do understand their pain, they desire this result so that they will not be hurt again and so that they can feel that others really do care. Only then can they *feel safe releasing their fear.* If those of us who have been wounded by life can find the courage to skip the necessity for others to feel our pain and simply choose to directly release our fear we can attain relief from our pain. Yet we often don't feel safe operating in this direct and bold a manner.

Of course, in our world it is not often feasible and it is obviously not socially acceptable (though many of us do try) to control other people in order to *cause them* the pain we have felt. Trying to do so actually results in our re-wounding our emotions and our own souls in a different way. This pain infliction dynamic is often seen in divorce proceedings that go on and on. In these cases spouses may be trying to variously prove themselves right, innocent or "the victim". In these situations one or both spouses may just want to punish the other. The end result is not positive for either spouse, whether emotionally or financially. The long term cost to any children involved is often even higher. It is possible to simply skip to the end of the process and release the fear and pain and save ourselves and those we love so much unnecessary difficulty.

Understanding that this is possible, feasible in the short term, and very worthwhile is the key to making it happen.

People who feel victimized can become so focused on their pain that they *forget how to heal* themselves and grow in a sovereign and independent manner. Again I am not pointing at this as a "fault". When we are wounded it is natural for us to focus on our pain and to seek help from others in dealing with it, and it is often necessary for us to be supported in our healing process. This is normal and there are many situations we could not recover from without this support. Still, in our healing process there comes a point where we must choose to independently work with our emotions and to become *internally motivated* to self-heal, if we are to successfully and fully transcend the pain of the past. If we choose to leave accountability for our lives or emotional process or our life results with anyone other than ourselves we only disempower ourselves. If we choose to place *all accountability* upon ourselves at some point in our healing journey (again *I am not suggesting blaming ourselves for the situation in any way*) then we optimally empower ourselves. I am suggesting empowering oneself by assuming that we all have the power to change anything in our lives for the better. Whether it be associated with our past, present or future, (*without any process of self-judgment or self-punishment through guilt or shame at all*). In this way we can fully empower ourselves and place all of the options for action on our own table, and all of the decisions in our own hands. This is an example of self-mastery and all of us have the potential to attain it at some point.

"*It is my right to feel the way I do and to identify myself as a victim for as long as I choose to because of all of the pain that I have been through*". Of course we all have free-will, and we can choose to feel any way that we choose to feel for as long as we choose to. It is a necessary part of our healing process for us to feel wounded and even to *temporarily* feel victimized. That said if victimhood or pain becomes an *identity* then it becomes a limitation on our capacity to heal, make conscious empowered decisions and to move on with our lives. Therefore it inhibits our ability to become who and what we want to become. In effect, in the long term, overt identification with victimhood robs us of our ability to find *inner peace*. This truth is not always apparent when we are at the beginning of the process of our trauma or woundedness. It may take years to get to the point where we can shift to another way of seeing past painful events, relationships, ourselves and life. I am not suggesting that anyone rush their process of healing. Like the process of grieving, all self-healing takes whatever time it takes. Child abuse, the most afflicting trauma I am aware of, may take much of a lifetime to work through. I am suggesting that with the application of tools of emotional release that the process may be shortened, and thereby that our time of pain can be reduced. Therefore our time of self-empowerment and joy can be hastened. This is my intention and my hope for the readers of this book.

By making all of the previous statements in this chapter I do not in any way excuse those who are perceived to be perpetrators for their choices, actions, beliefs or motivations, and I obviously do not condone negative or abusive behaviors or interactions between people in general. I am simply saying that if we hold any of the polarized perspectives of the V/P/R model or view of life to be true without deeper questioning then we can fall into a very large trap. This emotional reactive trap snares not only individuals; it also entangles families, groups, corporations, cultures, religions and whole nations. If we cannot extricate ourselves from the trap then we cannot heal, and we cannot make constructive decisions and take constructive actions.

Right now for example there are terrorist attacks occurring around the world, creating tremendous fear, pain and trauma and leaving many wounded, frightened and disillusioned people in their wake. Helping the world's people heal from these events rapidly, while effectively dealing with the problem of terrorism is important to the resolution of the problem. If we lose ourselves in fear, victimhood or hatred of the terrorists, or any other aspect of the Victim/Perpetrator/Rescuer dynamic, we will be less optimally capable of making wise decisions.

The latest understandings from experts are saying that we must intervene *socially* and insure that the people who could someday become terrorists never get to the point where they actually want to take this life path. *Children from all over the world, including from the United States* are making decisions to become terrorists and join factions such as the ISIS / ISIL terrorist group. Should we hate and want to destroy these lost children who are simply unwise, ignorant and buying into terrorist rhetoric or should we willfully and wisely choose to love them so much that we learn how to quickly help them to make more discerning decisions than to destroy themselves and others?

All terrorists were once children. Helping them means truly understanding what motivates them, helping them heal whatever is within them that could drive them to function as perpetrators/terrorists (usually some aspect of subconscious fear and thus their desire to be in control or more empowered in their lives) and then to help them to understand and clear this fear. This is a very different solution than simply making sure they have a good job, good economic conditions and an education. In today's increasingly complex and technologized world more people are becoming fearful, feeling disempowered, confused, disillusioned and angry. This is the source of terrorism, *its roots are fear*. Working with our children in this way is necessary so that their subconscious fears do not create a situation of vulnerability to their becoming entrained in terrorist rhetoric, negative emotional states, culture, identity and social dynamics. Again if we only hate and attack terrorists we will only make more hateful terrorists. If terrorists hate and kill us they will only motivate us to hate and kill them. Even terrorism, as extreme as it is, is not a black and white situation. Attempting to interpret terrorism as anything other than a *human situation* (no matter how barbarically it is acted out) keeps us from fully understanding it and effectively dealing with it.

Oddly enough it is even possible for us to see and feel ourselves to be victims of ourselves. This can be seen when we see ourselves as victims of our addictions, our desires, our negative emotions, our self-destructive actions, our fears of our own power, or our fears of the pain of our past choices that we cannot change. In these situations we can fear *our own power to cause ourselves pain without even realizing it*. It is necessary that we transcend our fear of our own capacity to hurt ourselves and to leave this tendency to fear ourselves behind permanently, if we want to feel confident and empowered in building joyful prosperous lives.

People who perceive themselves as victims may unwittingly become *perpetual victims* in various areas of their lives, as they project their past experiences as *future negative expectations* in regard to social interactions and relationships. In this case victimhood can become the underlying model for their whole way viewing of life, and this views necessity is constantly re-rationalized and re-validated and is thus rarely questioned. This need not be the case, the cycle of victimhood in individuals can be broken permanently and the larger V/P/R cycle in all of the world's cultures can be broken permanently. In order for this to occur our fear, our desire for control, and our tendency to judge ourselves and others must be given up. Fear is not a necessary part of life; it can be transcended with consciousness, wisdom, discernment and willful intention. If we choose to love ourselves and others unconditionally there will be no room for judgmentalness, fear, control or hatred.

So far we have shown how fear directly creates or supports all of the following detrimental situations:

- Negative emotions including hatred
- Relationship conflict and violence
- Judgmentalness and related punishment tendencies
- Prejudice, stereotyping and bias
- Addictions (in order to escape or manage the emotions of fear)
- Negative or limiting beliefs about ourselves, others, our relationships or the world, that result from fearful imaginings
- Expectations (fear creates fearful expectations of the future and fear is the resulting emotion of any of our expectations that are not met)
- Control seeking behavior in all relationships and situations
- Feelings of victimhood

Now we have added the V/P/R Model to the list of what fear creates and supports in terms of detrimental human conditions, dynamics, interactions and situations.

Chapter 17: Resolving Conflict in Relationships:

We have all had conflicts when trying to communicate and reach peaceful resolution of disputes in relationships. When we fear not getting what we want in relationships or fear being abandoned we often try to control situations and results and to control other's decisions and behaviors. We often do this by interrupting what others are saying or by criticizing or judging how they express themselves. When we do this it creates a whole new set of problems and conflicts. Whenever you find yourself in conflict in a relationship it is important to first understand what you fear most in the moment or in the future, and then simply immediately release that fear. At that point you will regain your perspective and see the situation more clearly for what it truly is. You will then become able and willing to negotiate for what you want consciously, fairly and wisely without trying to control or punish your partner for their point of view or way of being.

There are multitudes of fear driven destructive relationship dynamics that are all based in judgmentalness and which end in irreconcilable disagreement. Once this fear driven judgmental disagreement process has run its course it then leads to deep unreconciled *resentment*. This resulting resentment tends to fester in relationships over time and can turn to outright hatred if left unhealed. No one is truly ever either totally right or totally wrong in relationships. There are simply fear driven misunderstandings which lead to relationship negotiations going awry and which turn into conflict and control seeking in order to create a sense of personal safety or to achieve a personal desire.

As previously stated the main thing you are feeling when you feel fear is some form of projected potential for either emotional or physical abandonment or "death" or associated pain of loss, though you may not realize this in the moment. For example if you are afraid that you may be abandoned by your spouse then you may get caught up in requiring that your spouse prove that they are *NOT* going to abandon you. Therefore you may continually criticize them or punish them in some way in order to test their love for you. You may do this in order to continually get them to *prove that they won't abandon you.* Of course doing this will likely drive them farther away from you rather than draw them to you. Fear is not a functional decision-making process in relationships.

I use a metaphor to describe this dynamic I call "slapping the tiger". If you were walking through the jungle and happened upon a tiger you would likely obviously become frightened. In this situation the question I would pose would be how could you make *absolutely sure* the tiger would not eat you? An answer that our *irrational fears* could come up with is this. "Slap the tiger as hard as you can, then if it does not eat you, you can be sure you are safe." The only problem is that once you have slapped the tiger one time and it does not *immediately* eat you, your fears then say "how do I know it will not eat me in the next ten seconds?" Therefore our fears say, "I must slap the tiger again, just to be sure it will not eat me". You can see where this is going. In effect this is how our fears present themselves in our relationships. Meaning that when we feel insecure in a relationship we repeatedly try to test and retest those we fear hurting us emotionally, and try to make them "prove" that they are still trustworthy, and so in effect we "slap them" emotionally over and over. We do not realize that we are in effect hurting them and that this then may cause them to "slap us back" in resentment toward our testing process.

The main problem is that once they *do not* hurt us after we have slapped them our fears *do not go away* and our fears then continue to motivate us to get *fresh proof*. This skipping record sort of dynamic is a key reason why people have such ongoing problems in relationships; since *there is no way to prove to a fear that it is unwarranted* or unnecessary if it is being generated from an internal subconscious projection. This is by the way why paranoid people cannot be reasoned with, they are not seeing the person in front of them, they are seeing their own extreme fear projections to the exclusion of what is in front of them. This is also the reason why fears must be released internally and through some sort of release process, in order to fully and permanently resolve them. This type of fear driven testing dynamic creates many arguments and even fights in relationships and tends to continually undermine the process of constructive negotiation and resolution of issues of all kinds, in day-to-day life. It is hard to compromise with someone that you fear may hurt you emotionally.

If we want to transcend fear, control seeking, conflict, arguments, judgmentalness and even violence in relationships we must understand the roots of fear and how it affects relationship dynamics. We must also choose to release our fears if we want to cease falling into the traps of control seeking and judgmental criticism and punishment tendencies that fear creates in our relationships. The only way to live in peace in relationships is to place peace and love in relationships as our highest priority. Placing peace and love above fear is the imperative. Whether you are speaking of your own personal inner peace or creating peace between yourself and your spouse or peace between yourself and your children.

Chapter 18: Emotional Release Statements For Men in Relationships:

Men in almost every society have been taught to repress their emotions and to suppress their fear to one degree or another. For many this tendency is a key element of what might be termed "manliness". This tendency shuts men down to their emotional process and often leads to an inability on the part of men to feel when, where, how and why their subconscious fears are affecting their decisions and behaviors. This is why men become defensively angry and aggressive, without realizing that fear is driving their negative emotions. Anger and aggression are simply masks for underlying repressed fear that is not socially or personally acceptable to be felt or expressed.

Since men are not traditionally allowed socially to feel or express their fears, they are often unable to participate emotionally in various aspects of male/female relationship intimacy that require them to be more in touch with these aspects of their emotional process. Oddly enough many women who want men to be more intimate emotionally would not want their men to feel more fear, which of course is part of the problem. In addition, due to the increasing empowerment of women, which is dramatically escalating around the world, many men are experiencing extreme stress and anxiety in regard to their perceived role in their relationships. They are also unsure of just exactly what a man's social role is expected to be in today's world. This situation is creating a great degree of unresolved fear stress in men that again they do not feel safe expressing openly. In addition men have not traditionally been taught to manage their emotions as consciously as women have; therefore being open to their own emotions is new and unexplored territory for many men. There are few support systems in society at this time to help men with this exploration and learning process and little support for them to seek them out.

If we add the increasing pressure women are placing upon men to "get into their own emotions" and to be full and present emotional participants in relationships we can see that men are not having an easy time and that they are in need of tools for releasing reactive fear states. Men becoming empowered to release their own fears is a requirement if they are to then be able to feel safe getting into the gentler or more feminine aspects or parts of their emotional beings.

Below is a list of some suggested fear release statements which may help in regard to releasing relationship related fear stress, as well as other types of common fear stress that men today may encounter.

I am my fear of / that:

- I will be seen as weak if I show my fear
- I will be seen as unmanly if I show weakness, fear or vulnerability
- I will be seen as weak if I show uncertainty
- I will be seen as weak if I show that I do not know everything
- I will be seen as weak if I admit I am wrong
- I will be seen as weak if I ask forgiveness
- I will be seen as weak if I ask for guidance in regard to emotional issues from a woman
- I cannot meet my spouses/mates expectations
- my spouse may try to dominate or intimidate me
- my spouse may try to take advantage of my emotional vulnerability
- my spouse may manipulate me if I become vulnerable or show vulnerability
- my spouse will not respect me if I am emotionally vulnerable
- I cannot meet my own expectations in my relationship
- I am a failure in my relationship
- admitting that my spouse/mate knows more than I do in many areas of life
- admitting that my spouse/mate was right about something
- I cannot be the man that my spouse/mate wants me to be
- I cannot deal with the emotional pain of my relationship
- I cannot deal with spouse's/mates emotional pain
- I cannot meet my spouse's/mates emotional expectations
- I cannot meet my spouse's/mates intimacy needs
- I cannot meet my spouse's/mates sexual needs or expectations
- I cannot handle looking at my fears
- I others will not respect me if they find out I am afraid
- my wife/mate will not respect me if she finds out I am afraid
- I cannot open up about how I really feel
- if I open up about how I really feel I will be rejected or abandoned
- if I open up about how I feel I will be seen as weak, vulnerable or unmanly
- if I open up about how I feel I won't be seen as strong
- if I say how I feel I will only be criticized, rejected, judged or abandoned
- my inability to handle the problems in my relationship might lead us to divorce
- I am not in control in my relationship
- I fear my spouse/mate controlling me

- I fear my spouse/mate divorcing me and taking my children and all of my assets
- I am totally powerless in my relationship to control anything
- I do not understand what is going on in my relationship
- I do not understand my spouse/mate
- my relationship is broken and I do not know how to fix it
- my relationship is broken and I fear it is all my fault
- I am to blame for all the problems in my relationship
- if I do not support my family financially that I am not a man
- if I do not protect my family that I am not a man
- if I do not stand up to my wife I am not a man
- if I do not live my relationship the way I was taught by my parents that I am a failure
- if I do not control my spouse/mate they will control me
- I cannot emotionally trust my spouse
- my spouse may find someone else that they love or find more attractive than me
- my spouse only loves me for the support I offer
- my spouse does not truly love me
- if I lose my relationship that I will end up alone
- my spouse is right about all of her criticisms and judgments of me
- admitting that I lean on my spouse/mate just as much as she leans on me

I hope that these statements are useful in releasing your fears and that they can act as a springboard to finding other fears that you may have, that you can also release and thus free yourself from. Quality relationships make life worthwhile, and being our best selves within our relationships makes this quality possible. No one else can do it for us.

Chapter 19: Emotional Release Statements To Empower Women:

It is no secret that throughout human history women have been disempowered, disrespected and even openly abused by men, religions and societies. This history has left us with a situation of both conscious and subconscious fear in many women around the world of openly acting and speaking on their own behalf that is tragic, unjust, unfair and ultimately not to the benefit of any society or the world as a whole. I work with many women to help them transcend their fears in various areas of their lives, careers, relationships and in their process of spiritual consciousness development. Let me be clear, women are not victims; and I am not labeling them as such here. I see women as powerful and capable, and due to their emotional intelligence, potentially more intelligent, powerful and capable than men. What I am saying is that there are many women who have been unnecessarily affected by historical cultural tendencies and that this history can be effectively and positively changed for the better by releasing fear.

What I am about to describe is based upon many years of having worked with both men and women and helping them deal with their relationship issues. To even talk about gender bias can be to leave oneself open to being accused of having a bias of some sort. Taking any stance in regard to the complex, nuanced and relationship specific process of resolving the emotional and power issues between men and women is difficult. To work to empower women can be seen as a judgment or disempowerment of men. I have no judgment of men or their prior actions throughout history and I hope I am not interpreted in that way. Humanity has grown in the best way we have known how; to judge ourselves or our history serves no constructive purpose. To accurately understand ourselves and our history and to use this understanding to then make positive change does serve a purpose. My intention here is to ultimately facilitate peaceful and harmonious male / female understanding and to promote peace and balance of power between the genders around the world.

There are no generalities that fit every relationship nor are there generalities that fit every man or woman's life. That said I do feel that speaking of larger detrimental world trends and grossly obvious gender issues of imbalanced power and career financial rewards between men and women is very necessary and difficult to deny. Even more difficult to deny is the terrifying and horrifying record of physical and emotional abuse of, and rampant disempowerment of women by men, of women around the world. This situation has led many women to fundamentally emotionally fear and distrust men at both conscious and subconscious levels. This distrust directly affects the quality of male / female relationships. It often leads women to seek men as a source of security and safety and to simultaneously fear their destructive potential power.

There are many release statements that women I have worked with have found useful to release their fears and thus empower themselves in their interactions with men, and also with other women. Some of the women I have worked with have experienced direct physical or emotional abuse of various kinds at various stages of their lives. Most however have simply experienced the more insidious day-to-day undermining and limiting prejudice of the world's basic cultural, political and religious predispositions toward women or the emotional dismissal of male partners.

On the flip side of the relationship picture are the emotionally honorable and caring men who become overwhelmed by the sometimes overbearing emotional expectations of modern women. Some of these men may literally be emotionally battered in their inability to meet their mate's overly high expectations on an ongoing basis. Men today are expected to become proficient emotional partners, yet many have been given little or no training or support in the process of becoming aware of how to go about developing their emotional natures or their "feminine sides". This situation can be incredibly stress and fear producing for men and some may have no effective methods to manage their emotional stress as they gradually learn to emotionally interact with the women in their lives.

Speaking candidly men are often not as capable of effectively and openly communicating their emotional process as women are within the context of a dynamic and rapidly changing relationship. Many relationships today are highly transformational in nature as men and women try to define a whole new kind of relationship paradigm to replace old and outworn male/female roles that no longer serve. This can be a very intimidating situation for men, which can result in emotional shutdown or simple anger and frustration. Women can literally emotionally overwhelm men with their power to clearly verbalize their emotional perspectives in regard to their relationships, and thus "out communicate men" without realizing that this is occurring, and then resent men for not keeping up or for emotionally shutting down. Women may do so with the best of intentions or in great emotional desperation to make themselves and their needs understood. In either case two way communications are not optimally facilitated and thus relationship quality suffers and a history of misunderstanding is produced.

The reason I am discussing this situation in this way is because empowering women to communicate what they are truly feeling is not necessarily the complete solution to all relationship problems. Men may also need help and support in the process of opening themselves in order to be optimally able to communicate their emotions. Communication in relationships is always a two way street. Both partners in any relationship must be able to effectively communicate what they feel at all times in all situations. Therefore they must both have a way to feel safe at all times and thereby to be open to speak their truths as well as to fearlessly hear their partner's truths. It is equally important that women are receptive to the authentic emotional communications of their male partners. This mutually open state can be a difficult situation to achieve, especially if there is significant preexisting fear, pain, animosity or misunderstanding in the relationship, on either side. Oddly enough, many women are not as open as they may assume to hearing what their man really feels.

Around the world, in spite of all our implementations of laws and society's best efforts to counterbalance past detrimental traditions towards women, women are still being abused. Innate male tendencies to desire to control, dominate, manipulate, invalidate and even intimidate, coerce and abuse women are still pervasive; and there is still a tendency for women to be treated by men with less respect and less value than men treat other men. Women are still compensated in almost every profession in an unbalanced way in comparison to men. Women often do not feel safe expressing themselves in regard to this unjust situation, and this situation needs to change profoundly for the better, *now.* The release statements listed in this chapter, as well as similar statements that you can think up and design for yourself can be helpful in clearing your fears, and thereby open yourself to greater self-confidence, self-empowerment and self-sovereignty. When we practice facing our fears we eventually conquer our fears.

Some of the statements you will find listed in this chapter speak of the possibility of "harm" coming to women if they speak up publically or take direct action on their own behalf. Of course in day-to-day life *most women* would not be physically assaulted or punished if they were to openly speak their minds. However many women have the underlying *fear of some social or interpersonal reprisal* if they do openly speak their minds, even if it is not a true potential in the moment. I would by the way say the same of many men; it is simply our subconscious conditioning to be fearful of punishment, social abandonment, rejection and criticism that make us fearful. This fear can lead women to react with undesired self-imposed silence or self-edited communications in the work place, in relationships and in social situations.

Fear can also lead to situations of being or feeling dominated, invalidated and intimidated by male spouses, rather than women feeling safe to openly express themselves and their feelings, and thus women being empowered to negotiate on a level playing field for their emotional needs and what they want in relationships. Fear also leads to unreconciled problems in relationships because women do not feel safe expressing the "whole story" that they emotionally and intuitively understand to be true. Therefore relationship problems go on and on like skipping records due to a lack of being able to openly discuss them in clear and complete ways. Again the same can be true of men feeling "emotionally unsafe" and thus unable to discuss their own emotional process, feelings and reality. Women are not the only emotional creatures in the world; they are simply *usually* somewhat more emotionally self-knowledgeable and self-involved with their emotions than *most* men. Again this is not a black and white situation, and there are obviously many loving and highly emotional men in the world for which I have great respect. We are only speaking here of those men who have not yet achieved this state of emotional self-awareness, understanding and function.

The conscious and subconscious fears that some women have can lead to the *expectation* of being censored by men or even other women in the work place or socially, which then leads to unrealized *preventive self-censorship*. In other words, some women try to save themselves from what they fear could happen to them socially by preventively censoring themselves, *before* they can be socially punished for speaking up. Men do this too, just not as often or in the same situations or in the same manner. This is in many ways the human condition and is a *fear based decision-making process* rather than one that is based upon deeply conscious and accurate understanding of work place situations, social situations or personal relationships. These *projected fears* are truly not beneficial and create vast limitations on our *perceived safe options* and thus our potential to powerfully create the lives, relationships and careers that we want to create.

Women are every bit as intelligent as men; this is a simple fact. That said, women may not always be as confident in their abilities, or as supported by society, their families, their organizations or their cultures in the pursuits of their dreams as some men are. There is even a cultural myth that men are somehow "smarter, better or more capable in general than women". This is totally false and is sometimes competitively propagated by men to *preemptively undermine* women's goals, desires, values and perspectives. Men and women are different in some ways, both have their strengths and capabilities, both are valuable, both deserve to be treated equally. It is common knowledge that women are often required to work harder than men in the work place to prove their worth.

There are many different types of intelligence, some of them are emotional intelligence, some are associated with creativity and some are social and relationship intelligence. In many areas of life *some* women are often far more functionally capable than *some* men. Though many men may be loath to accept this fact due to the emotional vulnerability they feel when they face such realizations. Women are often better at multi-tasking and are generally far better communicators than men. Women are also generally better at emoting, and understanding and managing the complex and subtle nature of social and interpersonal relationships than men. It is these potential blind spots in some men's understanding and capacity to process these types of subtle social and emotional information which makes men unable to acknowledge, respect and revere the capabilities of women. This lack of understanding makes men unwilling to reward women appropriately, both financially and in terms of mutual respect.

Men also *often* (not always) have a fundamentally different set of values than women. Men process the information of their life experience differently than women (i.e. less emotionally and less *relationally*). Therefore men's value systems often do not match up to women's and therefore men do not have a way to appropriately value women's perspectives, values and decisions in relationships or in business environments. They also do not always share values when working in teams in the work place.

Simply put, men often cannot clearly perceive and understand the subtle emotion based skills women possess in order to accurately "measure them". Because of this men cannot appropriately place value on them. Because of this men cannot understand how to "design in" women's soft skills into organizational functions; therefore men cannot make use of women at executive levels to optimize organizational functions. Therefore men cannot adequately prioritize and assign value to these complex social skills in the work place and in organizational decision-making processes as a whole! Therefore the solutions that women could come up with in the organization are not arrived at and the problems they could solve in a completely different way than a man would, remain unsolved.

I have observed and counseled male / female relations for many years. From this study it is my perception that in the core of the collective male ego and psyche, men subconsciously assume that they have *all the answers* that are needed to every problem, and can *or must* figure out the answers they need in every situation. They want to achieve this *without feminine interaction or support unless it is in a subservient role.* Any other form of interaction with women in a working situation, (i.e. equal partnership, mutually respectful teamwork, or even subservience to a female boss) does not support egoic male self-images of competitive dominance and thus personal safety. Therefore when interacting with women in a decision-making situation, such as in a work situation, they "instinctively and conveniently feel" that women's input is not needed *or desired* in order to solve problems or make decisions. This is the source of the behavior on the part of men that women would often refer to as "Mansplaining" where men dismissively condescend to women, interrupt them and attempt to come off as knowing everything. In the business world this subconscious tendency for men to remain in their comfort zones creates a fatal assumption and a huge waste of our valuable female human resources. If this flawed reasoning is followed, it excludes women from key decision-making roles and all high level executive positions and consistently relegates them to lower positions in the organization. If you look at how most of the world is operating you can see that this is exactly what has been happening for a very long time, and that this attitude on the part of men is a significant reason why it has been happening. It is time for this to stop. Male "over competitiveness" for the sake of attaining control, and thereby monopoly over finances is unbalancing and therefore over time destroying our world. Competitiveness for the goals of *control and power* is driven not by strength or wisdom, but by insecurity and fear. What we need is complete and consistent gender equality, harmony, mutual respect and understanding and balance.

Because of the above listed situations organizations suffer from a lack of soft skills being optimally implemented on a consistent basis at all levels and in all areas of the organization due to male's incapacity to understand them. This is the essence of and reason for the "glass ceiling" that many women face in organizations when they seek advancement, and why men feel threatened by women. In essence men cannot understand or predict when, where, how or why women will function and make decisions as they do. Women may thus labeled "overly emotional or irrational" simply because men cannot understand and appreciate their process. Therefore women's decisions and behavior trigger men's fear of not being in control, and thus men feel unsafe (though most men would likely not state it in these terms), therefore men want to remain dominant and in control of women in organizations. Therefore men who run organizations underutilize the powerful and skilled women that populate their organizations.

These subtle social skills are foundational to what could be termed or seen as the larger and more sophisticated capability of "women's intuition", which men often do not have a way to recognize, categorize, value, measure, compete against or reward. Women's decision-making is often scoffed at as irrational, illogical, or being too prone to the influence of erratic feminine emotion to be reliable. This is gender bias at its worst and creates a social and organizational climate of subconscious prejudice toward feminine decision-making which women *may* either consciously or subconsciously react to with fear and self-censorship. So there remains an unreconciled "understanding gap" and communications gap in the work place between men and women, which translates into *a power gap and a financial reward gap*. For this reason women are forced to outperform men just to gain acceptance in the workplace and to be considered equal, while not being rewarded equally. This job disparity is currently being faced most acutely in the technology sector, which is heavily male dominated, to its detriment. The reason that the core of this problem remains obscured is the unresolved and "undiscussible" subconscious fear on both sides, (both male and female), as well as a lack of a standard process to effectively and efficiently deal with it. (Let's face it folks, does the average person want to face their deepest fears of rejection and abandonment if they are not required to by some obvious threatening problem in their lives?)

In essence men wish to strongly compete, succeed and dominate in the work place and in the world and do not want to bring emotional vulnerability into the corporate or work environment. Because men often do not know how to recognize, value and *properly implement* "soft skills" in the work place they do not recognize when they are acting in an insensitive, intimidating, disrespectful or dismissive fashion toward women. Due to simple subconscious fear, ignorance, and base competition for power and personal success in the workplace many men are *not motivated to want to implement women's capabilities in the workplace*. In many corporate cultures what passes for being a "team player" is actually simple submission to the status quo of a male dominated executive culture. *Actual teamwork*, especially teamwork in a balanced and mutually respectful manner between men and women, with truly balanced compensation, is almost unknown to most corporate cultures. Women and their mastery of these soft skills have tremendous potential benefit to the work place and to the world as a whole and this situation needs to change now, for the good of all.

The feared potential social and personal reprisals or consequences women face daily can run the gambit from:

Fear of:

- being judged on a different scale or by a different set of standards than men in the work place
- social and personal abandonment if they express their personal power
- diminishment of the quality of their relationships if they express their personal power
- excessive loss of perceived social status or social value if they make a mistake
- overt gender focused criticism if they express their personal power
- potential direct expressions of male condescension, intimidation, anger, expressions of "emotional violence and rejection" or even physical violence if they express their personal power
- being called a "bad mother" if they appear to focus on their career more than on their role of mother
- male emotional rejection if they choose to act independently of men's desires, expectations or views
- having their thoughts, views or ideas openly mocked, or called "irrational, illogical, emotional, not based in fact or stupid" by men
- being called out publically by men to ridicule them into submission rather than holding a supportive space for their ideas to be fairly reviewed and fully understood
- being "hurt" by men if they stand up for themselves (the word "hurt" is not specifically defined here, yet I am sure that many women can relate to it very well). The hurt feels real, whether it is emotional or physical
- embarrassment by men
- being made fun of or not being taken seriously by men
- being made less than by men
- being called a "bitch" if the woman stands up for herself or does not function in a support role to a man
- being called or seen as non-feminine if she is assertive or competitive
- being seen by others as less than perfect

Some suggested release statements designed to empower women are the following:

I am my fear:

- that men will not respect what I have to say or the work that I do
- of what others will think of how I have used my power
- of being powerful
- of being powerless
- of being a victim
- of being or appearing weak or vulnerable to attack
- of saying "the wrong thing"
- that I am just a woman alone in a man's world
- of men are more powerful than I am
- of being wrong
- of not being right
- of my own power
- of misusing my power
- of not doing things the right way
- of being judged or punished for not doing things the right way
- that men will not validate, value or reward the efforts I put out or work I do
- that men will not listen to me
- that men do not appreciate me
- that men do not respect me as a person
- that I will not be rewarded for my efforts
- that men will not value, respect or even *understand me* or what I want
- that I do not matter to men and how I feel does not matter to them
- that if I speak up I will be silenced by men
- that if I speak my truth it will not be listened to by men
- that if I speak my truth I will be silenced, threatened or even attacked
- that men will abuse me or use me
- that men assume I am only here to support them
- that men will not take me, my work or my ideas seriously
- that men do not value me or what I have to say or what I do
- that what I have to say is not important or that others do not feel that what I have to say is important
- that what I have to say is not as good, right or as "intelligent" as what a man might say
- that men will deny my emotions and what I have to say if I speak about my emotions
- that I am not good enough
- that I am not perfect enough
- that men will only value me physically attractive and not value me if I am mentally capable

- that men will be threatened by me if I show how smart I am or how much I know
- that men will reject me if I show how smart I am or how much I know
- that men will reject me or attack me if I say how I feel or express my emotions
- that men will invalidate or disregard my emotions and feelings
- of being criticized
- of being called emotional or irrational
- of what other's will think of me
- of being a "bad mother" or being accused of being a bad mother
- of being wrong or making mistakes
- of saying something "stupid"
- that "they" will think I am a "just being a bitch"
- that they will say I am "too emotional"
- of what others will say about me
- of what others will think about me
- of what others will feel about me
- that I won't be "wanted" if I am competitive or assertive

I hope it is obvious that this list is just the tip of the *fear iceberg*. People's fears are specific to their lives, their situations and their relationships and can be triggered at any moment. Having the opportunity to clear away barriers to your progress in all areas of your life is empowering. Admitting that you have barriers is empowering, and is the first step in transcending them.

Chapter 20: What We Can All Do to Resolve World Conflicts:

Our fears become recorded along with our experiences in our systems along with our pain. Our fears become projected into our present and onto our imaginings of the future. We sometimes pump so much energy into our fearful projections that they crystalize into fear based negative beliefs about ourselves, others and the world. When we interpret our life experiences through the filter or lens of our fearful projections then we create memories tainted by fear, which over time also tend to produce a database of fearful memories which feed the production of fear based beliefs. The fear based belief creation process is self-perpetuating and self-distorting. It has a "snowball effect" over time and across our life time. We can, without realizing it, gradually spiral downward into a more and more fearful attitude toward life. This same process can happen to individuals and to groups and to nations. We use our fears as values, among our other values, to make our decisions and in so doing to create our beliefs and our belief systems. We use our beliefs and belief systems to create our life strategies. Countries may use their belief systems to formulate national policy and military or economic strategy. Our fears often trump all of our other values without our even realizing that it has happened. This insidious process can slowly evolve over time and undermine the very foundation of trust between individuals, groups and nations. All the while we are rationalizing why it is necessary to remain safe and secure and validating when, where, how and why we are digging ourselves deeper into our fear and why it is necessary to destroy the quality of open communications and loving interpersonal trust with others. No wonder we have difficulty working together in committed faith, integrity and trust to solve the world's problems.

Sometimes we become gridlocked in our decision-making due to the process of our many fears trumping our other values, which also represent our other life motivations and decision-making criteria. Usually we can only have the gridlock broken when a much worse "trumping fear" occurs. When we see through the lens of fear what we see is not reality. We see only what we project and this keeps us from seeing the real problems that we are dealing with clearly, and this renders us unable to solve them appropriately and directly.

When we look at global problems we can see that many global problems remain unresolved because large groups of people or nations continue to look at situations through the lens of fear, pain of the past or through the lens of negative or limiting beliefs. It is the release of these fears, pains, and limiting or negative beliefs that frees us all to change the world profoundly, and thereby to create new and wonderful potential futures.

Without these types of mental and emotional releases occurring on a *large scale*, meaning on the scale of populations, we will likely remain limited by our past views, to our national and global detriment. It is my hope that leadership will find the conscience and motivation to guide us to the necessary understandings and consciousness to allow us all to release the pain of the past so that we may embrace our positive potential as a world community.

In order to achieve this goal, it is my perception that globally teaching a standardized method of releasing fear, past pain and negative and limiting emotions and detrimental beliefs is necessary. I also believe it is possible to develop and teach a new and more functional system of human interaction dynamics. A system that is not based upon fear, judgment, punishment or negative emotional dynamics as our current systems are. This new system would include methods of managing consciousness and negative emotions, as well as teaching new more functional and optimal life and relationship decision-making strategies. It is only through learning to function in more self-aware ways that we can learn to manage ourselves and our relationships better and learn to make better decisions in general. I believe that if such a system of standardized methods were made available via the internet that it would empower people everywhere to free themselves from the limitations of the historically detrimental aspects of the traditional and often negative drama oriented human emotional process. It could also facilitate a massive shift in consciousness that is needed if we want the world's people to be better prepared to deal with the massive technological, political, economic and ecological changes that are already happening and will only continue to escalate. If we want our children to be able to optimally manage their lives in an increasingly complex world in the future it is vital that we give them the tools to optimally manage their emotional wellbeing now.

Motivating world leaders and educators to provide such systems *now* on a mass scale is necessary if we want this problem to be handled in the near term. We all have a vote in this process; we all have power and influence. If we choose to we can put in place globally available systems that will facilitate and support the ongoing development and evolution of all of humanity and this can occur very rapidly. Such systems could teach people to live their lives without fear, negative emotional dynamics, judgement, prejudice, detrimental relationship dynamics, religious or racial intolerance or destructive tendencies. If we do nothing then what is happening now will continue and will likely get worse. If we assume that someone else will take care of these problems and that we need do nothing it is likely that things will get worse. None of the current systems that are currently in place in the world are adequate to the task. Our current educational systems, systems of governance, systems of managing mental illness, systems of facilitating individual's emotional development (i.e. the family) are all falling far behind the curve when it comes to dealing with the problems listed in this book. We can do far better. We can do better if we choose to do better. For the sake of future generations we must do better.

Chapter 21: Resolving Your Safety and Control Strategies:

We all have what I term Safety Strategy Beliefs. These are simple yet powerfully entrenched subconscious beliefs that we have used all of our lives to keep ourselves safe, yet which are ultimately limiting, dysfunctional and often self-defeating. Though they are usually subconscious, they affect every area of our lives and relationships. They are usually based in false beliefs in absolute states of complete control, complete safety, or in the possibility of being completely accepted by others. None of which can really occur for any length of time in real life. All of these beliefs are just ego self-defense strategies designed to keep us feeling physically safe or safe from feeling abandoned emotionally. Examples of these safety strategy beliefs are:

- I am only safe if I am in control of everyone in my life
- I am only safe if I am in control of my emotions
- I am only safe if I am perfect all the time
- I am only safe if I am needed
- I am only safe if I know more or better than everyone else
- I am only going to be safe and happy if I am married
- I am only safe if *everyone* accepts me
- I am only safe if I am tough, strong and suppress my emotions
- I am only safe if I am the one in power or authority
- I am only safe if I am right
- I am only safe if I am free to criticize / abandon / judge / punish / hurt / harm or kill others in my own defense
- I am only safe if I a success
- I am only safe if I am a success and if I make a lot of money
- I am only acceptable if I have a great job
- I am only a man if I provide for my family
- I am only successful if I am married
- I am only safe if I am a winner

These safety and control oriented beliefs supposedly help us to manage our lives and to stay safe. At the same time they create conflict in our relationships every time we follow them. They simultaneously and repeatedly create vast fear, stress, limitation and self-expectation in various areas of one's life. They create this because they are unrealistic and cannot be achieved in reality, therefore they constantly *trigger the very fear* they are designed to try to manage or suppress. They also create this situation because we have associated these beliefs with our physical or emotional survival, which is an intense emotional motivation that is not truly satisfied by the belief strategy we are trying to apply.

Releasing these beliefs and the associated fear that drives them frees us from the limitations they impose on our lives and relationships, and thus opens us to new and unforeseen creative opportunities. It is sometimes difficult to see through the falsehood of these beliefs and to become motivated to give up our key safety strategies. Still it is important that we do so in order to free our creativity and our *conscious power* and to thereby be fully open to love, intimacy and happiness, and free from fear and associated control seeking.

Statements that can help to free us from these types of safety related fear beliefs are:

- "I am my fear that" I am only safe if I am in control of everyone in my life
- "I am my fear that" I am only I am only safe if I am in control of my emotions
- "I am my fear that" I am only safe if I am perfect all the time
- "I am my fear that" I am only safe if I am needed
- "I am my fear that" I am only safe if I know more or better than everyone else
- "I am my fear that" I am only going to be happy if I am married
- "I am my fear that" I am only safe if *everyone* accepts me
- "I am my fear that" I am only safe if I am tough, strong and suppress my emotions
- "I am my fear that" I am only safe if I am the one in power or authority
- "I am my fear that" I am only safe if I am right
- "I am my fear that" I am only safe if I a success
- "I am my fear that" I am only safe if I am a success and if I make a lot of money
- "I am my fear that" I am only acceptable if I have a great job
- "I am my fear that" I am only a man if I provide for my family
- "I am my fear that" I am only successful if I am married
- "I am my fear that" I am only safe if I am a winner

Working with these types of statements, over time, can reduce the detrimental and limiting effects of these deeply engrained safety strategies, even if they have been influencing you for a lifetime at subconscious levels. It is likely that shedding these beliefs will help you tremendously in every area of your life and in all of your relationships.

Chapter 22: Breaking Free of The Prison of Your Comfort Zone:

We all have comfort zones that we like to stay, live and work within in the various areas of our lives. We may not realize just what it is that comprise these comfort zones, what the actual cost is of living within these zones, or what the implications of living within them are. Our comfort zones are areas of well-known and understood relationships, decision-making, behavior and expected life results. We as individuals usually feel uncomfortable or even frightened when we step out of our comfort zones. This is because at the edge of our comfort zones we find the beginning of our two *fear zones which surround* our comforts zones.

Our first fear zone is made up of what "we know we fear" or imagine we should or will fear, and is all made up of our imagined projections and includes our subconscious fears. Beyond this zone of fear is our second fear zone which is the less realized realm of our fear and is simply made up of our fear of the *unknown,* which is something we all instinctively fear. We fear the unknown because by the very definition of it, it cannot be controlled, because it is unknown, unrealized, undefined and therefore there is no way to prepare for it, apply any power, force or control onto it. Therefore the unknown has the potential to trigger any version and intensity of both of our main fears of death and abandonment. Rapid or extreme changes in our lives tend to trigger this fear since we can never know how this kind of change may affect our lives or how it may ultimately unfold in our lives or affect others in our lives.

Operating from within our comfort zones tends to limit our learning, experiences, understanding, options, free-will choice and thus the results of all of our endeavors. We tend to obscure the existence of our fear zones from our consciousness even as we focus on our comfort zones, to our detriment. Certainly it is more comfortable to stay within the range of the known and the comfortable, and that which does not trigger our fears, however doing so renders our lives less than they can be. There are many joys and wonders in life that we cannot experience until we are ready and willing to push beyond the limits of our comfort zones. Our fear zones are actually zones of opportunity and growth!

In addition to the fear zones of individuals, large groups, organizations and even nations all have *operational comfort zones,* and they all also have these two surrounding fear zones. These fear zones are usually "undiscussible topics" for most people, organizations and nations because to discuss them openly would show fear, vulnerability or potential weakness that would be unacceptable. This fear of showing fear and vulnerability is a key reason why positive change on a large scale within corporations, within nations and between nations around the world is difficult to bring about.

The boundaries of the comfort zones for organizations and nations are usually defined by rules, policies and strong cultural boundaries and limiting fear based beliefs. The fear zones that surround these comfort zones are not talked of as fear zones; they may be seen as "risk management" zones or potential problem zones for various reasons. Yet in the end they evoke fear in the group members, executive management of the organization or policy makers of the nation. These fear zones are the main reasons that corporations are not more free, innovative and creative places. Allowing unfettered freedom, innovation and creativity would trigger too much fear of loss of control and evoke a fear based control seeking response by management. This reaction would be designed to shut down the "ungoverned and thus fear producing process of creativity" before it got out of hand.

I am not criticizing organizations or corporations, I am describing fundamental human fear dynamics and how they tend to unfold in groups of people, in the work place and in nations. These dynamics are so engrained and fundamental to human interaction that all of us are unconsciously influenced by them, whether we are executives, managers, employees or politicians. It is vital that we understand these dynamics and their influence on decision-making at all levels of organizations if we want to improve the lot of all of humanity.

Any situation that involves profound change or the seeming potential for profound risk in a corporation tends to trigger the fear control response of the organization. Usually because they have stockholders and investors who are risk adverse, or because stepping outside the organization's comfort zone might affect perceived control over the reward process or power structure of the organization's elite, or it may trigger executive's individual ego self-defense mechanisms. Employees within the organization are expected to resonate with the fears of the larger organizational consciousness if they are to participate in the organization, even if the organization does not fundamentally or empathetically care about its employees. This compliance is often deemed necessary for employees to "prove loyalty" to the organization as well as to insure the safety of the organization, sometimes even over and above the safety of the individual employee. There *are* many caring organizational cultures in the world that are very conscious and employee value centric, I am not speaking here of those more conscious organizations.

In all top down command and control style organizational power structures there is a fundamental mistrust and thus degree of fear on the part of management in regard to the quality of decision-making of the people in the lower levels of the organization. This is an often unrealized elitist bias which is all too common among leadership today. This bias limits humanities' options globally in terms of organizational design, development and quality of operation. This fear/mistrust tendency directly limits employee creativity, innovation, empowerment, open organizational communication, teamwork, trust building and thus the achievement of broader organizational goals. Certainly hierarchically designed organizations have their advantages from a practical efficiency vantage point. Still there are other potential ways we can work together in groups which are far more open and trust based and which have greater potential to bring open communication, creativity and innovation rapidly and consistently into our day to day business reality. With these changes can come greater employee fulfillment and empowerment.

The flip side of the fear equation is the fear and mistrust that employees have of their management. Employees fear not being cared about, being punished, criticized, mislead by management, not attaining their career goals, being fired for not meeting their employer's expectations, or being punished for not meeting the expectations of their organization's culture. These fears create limitations on individuals causing them to be less trusting, creative, innovate, communicative and team oriented. In addition, the focus on competition that pervades many corporate environments creates a fear and mistrust of one's own work mates and fundamentally undermines the necessary process of trust-building that supports teamwork. These larger dynamics of fear are destructive to all of us as individuals and detrimental to the function of organizations in general.

If we as individuals or as organizations, large groups or nations clear the fear zones that surround our comfort zones then we expand our comfort zones and with them our conscious options in terms of how we think, feel, act and develop. It is the process of releasing fears from our fear zones in a conscious, wise, constructive, methodical and comprehensive manner which accomplishes this expansion of the comfort zone and empowers us to be able to constructively and creatively change ourselves and the world for the better. The surrounding fear zones are often believed to be necessary, because of the inaccurate assumption that our fears are what keep us safe. Of course fears do not keep us safe, they only keep our consciousness, our awareness and our options encumbered. Unfortunately the only way for people, groups or nations to realize this fact is for them to *first transcend their fears*. Until they do so their consciousness will remain obscured by their fears. Until we are ready to face our fears and admit that we are functioning from a position of fear we are usually unwilling to transcend our fear. It is the fear based decision-making tendencies of organizations which create the apparent "soulless" or non-empathetic process of operation and decision-making of many corporations. This tendency can be changed for the better.

What I am suggesting is that we all (individuals and groups) have the capacity to consciously manage our life limiting comfort zones and to expand them limitlessly and rapidly; in fact they can be expanded to the point where we fear no threats at all. This does not mean that we will be unaware of real or existing threats or that we are rendered unable to deal with them effectively, in fact we actually become far more conscious and powerful when we release our fears. It only means we do not deal with threats reactively and from the *lowest level of conscious capability*, (i.e. from reactive fear, mistrust and ignorance). If you are seeking more information about how organizations can be better designed and function optimally you may find the following book of interest. Reinventing Organizations, By Frederic Laloux.

My suggestion is that it is essential and valuable to understand that you have a comfort zone and surrounding fear zones in every area of your life and relationship and that you can learn to rapidly manage and transcend it all. If you do so then you can become far more capable and empowered than you ever dreamed you could be. If you choose not to do so then you will remain in your comfort zone and remain limited and your life unchanged. I will respect your choice, as I see it as and respect it as your free-will. If you choose to methodically map and release your fears and transcend them all then you can change *everything about your life*, including who you think you are, where you will go in life, what you will do, what you will experience, who you will love, who will love you, what you will know and what dreams you will manifest. It is your choice to make. I wish you the best in this process.

Shakespeare wrote "To be or not to be, that is the question". I would suggest that you can say to yourself "To be and live a Sovereign, Conscious, Free and Fearless life *or not* to truly be, that is the question." It is a choice you are making in every moment of your life whether you realize it or not. You can awaken now forever or fall back asleep. I can tell you that your fears prefer that you sleep rather than awaken and live.

Chapter 23: Manifesting What You Want Most In Your Life:

We all want to create or manifest wonderful lives of joy and happiness. At the same time we fear many things along the way. Whenever we want someone we love to love us, we also tend to fear their rejection or potential abandonment. Whenever we envision a dream we want to achieve we simultaneously and subconsciously fear all of the possible scenarios that could inhibit us in the process of realizing it. It is the distraction and interference of these unnecessary fear projections that often keep us from realizing our dreams in day-to-day life.

Most of us live our lives like a person looking out across a vast empty field. In front of us on this field we see our beautiful dreams shining in the distance. At the same time between us and our dreams we subconsciously project the ghostly images of every fearful possibility we imagine could occur on the way to our dreams. Then as we live our lives we spend our time bobbing and weaving, leaping and jumping to and fro, trying to avoid and escape from the fearful images we have projected as we pursue our dreams. None of the fearful projections exist, only what we do *now* does exist, and only what we do *now* helps us create the life we really want and the dreams we envision. Still each fearful projection can appear to us to be real and the more we focus on it, and the more energy we put into it, the more real it seems, and the more energy we waste avoiding it.

Unfortunately some of us put so much energy into our fears we end up *creating our fears* in our lives, instead of our dreams, and then we wonder how it all happened. For example the fear that we will never be loved for who we really are may appear to some of us to be very real, and even be supported by our experiences. Yet the fear that we will never be loved is only a false fear and it only has the substance we pour into it through the energy of our focus on it. We must clear the fear and pain of past experiences, and cease to put energy into them. Then we can make room for others to love us for who we are and we will cease to impede them from loving us in the present. If we are busy fearing we are literally unwilling to allow others to actually love us, because we are fearing that they will not, so in our fear we will not allow them to get close enough to us to love us.

It is helpful to understand and *map our overall systems of fear* and understand how they affect our process of manifesting out dreams and desires in life. Just focusing on "positive outcomes" consciously will not clear all of our subconscious fears. Because in effect we will be in a tug of war with the fears in our subconscious while we are consciously trying to manifest our positive dreams. We must clear our fears AND focus on positive outcomes. A way to map your fears is to focus on anything that you want very much in life and then to focus on all the fears that you have *around that desire*, and then to *clear the fears*, and then work to manifest your dream *without the fears*. For example choose something you dream of having in your life, then list all your fears relating to:

- not having your dream or living life without it (whether your dream is a goal, job, money, relationship, object, or a situation)
- what it will take in terms of your effort to make your dream happen
- what it will take to keep it once you do make it happen
- the possibility of losing it once you do have it
- what others will think of you for having it
- how others might try to take it from you
- how much it will cost
- how much time it will take to manifest it
- how you will feel about yourself for manifesting it
- how you will feel about yourself if you fail to attain your dream
- how others will feel about you if you have your dream
- how your identity will change if you have your dream
- how your identity will change if you lose your dream

After learning what your fears are, then create a list of statements to release each fear. As in:

- "I am my fear that it will cost too much to have the house I want"
- "I am my fear that I will be rejected if I ask the man/woman I want to marry me"
- "I am my fear that I am not smart enough to start my own business"
- "I am my fear that I will am just not good enough to be the CEO of my own company"
- "I am my fear that I won't be a good parent if I choose to have children"
- "I am my fear that I will lose my future spouse if I choose to get married to her/him"
- "I am my fear that if I become a manager my work friends won't talk to me anymore"
- "I am my fear that if I am a big success that I won't know who I am anymore"

There is a statement you can create to describe any fear that you have; therefore there is a solution to any fear. You need only *carve the key* to the particular lock in the door that is barring you from your dreams.

Conclusion:

We all have vast power; we are all creating our own lives continually through our free-will choices, even if we do not realize it as we are doing it. It is our choice whether we do it unconsciously through fear or through conscious sovereign willful wisdom and discernment. The "engine of the world" and of humanity's development and evolution runs on *emotional fuel.* Everyone in the world, as individuals, make choices every day, and in every moment, as to which emotional fuel we will run our lives on, and thus what the world will run upon.

Our *emotional fuel* colors, limits or defines every decision we make each day and thus directly affects the results of every choice we make. We can choose to run our lives and the world on fear and all of its negative destructive emotional reflections, or we can run our lives on joy, love, gratitude, trust, open communication, compassion and hope. I believe that you can tell for yourself and from the information included in this book which fuel is the more optimal choice. I hope that the information in this book serves you on your path to manifesting your dreams and in releasing any and all fears that impede you from having whatever it is that you most desire in your life. I wish you all the best in fearlessly manifesting and living your dreams.

Appendix To Chapter 8:

Appendix A: Emotional Self-Analysis

The following statements are designed to elicit unconscious or subconscious emotional responses, answers, information and self-understanding. The result of the process of completing these sentences is a method of finding unhealed or misunderstood parts of yourself so you can work with them. You may find several answers to each statement, this is fine, and each is worth contemplating. Mark off each item with a pencil as you go. Journaling as you go is suggested.

Once you have identified these unconscious beliefs, feelings and programs you can use various methods discussed in the book to release them and to be free of previously limiting beliefs, emotions and attitudes.

Please finish the following statements:

1. ○ I feel the most angry when ...
2. ○ My greatest fear is ...
3. ○ I feel the most guilty when ...
4. ○ I feel the most ashamed when ...
5. ○ My greatest emotional pain is ...
6. ○ The emotion I most want to deny is ...
7. ○ I most need to heal my ...
8. ○ The event in life that hurt me the worst was ...
9. ○ The person I most need to forgive is ...
10. ○ The person I blame the most is ...
11. ○ The thing I regret the most is ...
12. ○ I wish I hadn't ...
13. ○ If I could do it over again I would ...
14. ○ I'll never forgive myself for ...
15. ○ I will never forgive (*Insert person's name here)* for ...
16. ○ People should never ...
17. ○ I should never ...
18. ○ I should always ...
19. ○ I must always ...
20. ○ I must never ...
21. ○ I have to ...
22. ○ I was treated the most unfairly by ...

23. ○ I hate it when …
24. ○ I hate people who …
25. ○ I get afraid when …
26. ○ I get angry when …
27. ○ I feel guilty when …
28. ○ I don't trust people when …
29. ○ I don't trust people who …
30. ○ I blame myself for …
31. ○ I blame my mother for …
32. ○ I blame my father for …
33. ○ I blame my husband / wife for …
34. ○ I feel the need to apologize for …
35. ○ I feel weak when …
36. ○ I felt betrayed when …
37. ○ I felt abandoned when …
38. ○ I felt powerless when …
39. ○ I feel the most when …
40. ○ When I say I love myself I feel …
41. ○ When I say I am powerful I feel …
42. ○ When I say I am free I feel …
43. ○ When I say I am honest I feel …
44. ○ When I say I deserve to be loved I feel …
45. ○ When I say I deserve to have a wonderful happy life I feel…
46. ○ When I say I am safe and secure in the world I feel …
47. ○ When I say my heart is open and loving I feel …
48. ○ When I say my father loves me I feel …
49. ○ When I say my mother loves me I feel …
50. ○ The person I am most dependent upon is …
51. ○ The person I am most responsible for is …

Appendix B: Belief System Analysis

Please read the unfinished sentences below. Then, after looking deeply into your own thoughts and feelings about each, write out all the most meaningful "completions" to the sentences.

For example the first sentence below: "I believe in ..." could be finished in this way.
"I believe in loving others more than I believe in loving myself."

You may get several answers to each incomplete sentence as you review your various feelings about the sentence; this is fine, they are all important in the ongoing process of understanding yourself. Journaling as you work through the list is suggested.

Whatever meaningful answers, feelings or information arise from your emotions and your subconscious upon contemplation of the sentences are part of your inner world. They are all worth understanding. The answers you arrive at are often what you base your interpretations of your experience of life and relationships upon (consciously or unconsciously), and in turn your life decisions. These interpretations and their associated decisions powerfully affect the results that you attain in your life endeavors.

General beliefs:

1. ○ I believe in ....
2. ○ I believe I am ....
3. ○ I believe people are ....
4. ○ I believe men are ...
5. ○ I believe women are ...
6. ○ I believe children are ...
7. ○ I believe bosses are ...
8. ○ I believe employees are ...
9. ○ I believe wives are ...
10. ○ I believe husbands are ...
11. ○ I believe my mother is ...
12. ○ I believe my father is ...
13. ○ I can believe in something when ...
14. ○ I can believe in someone when ...
15. ○ I can change a belief when ...
16. ○ I hold onto beliefs because ...
17. ○ I quit believing in something when ...
18. ○ I believe in myself when ...
19. ○ I quit believing in myself when...

Beliefs about relationships:

1. ○ I believe relationships are …
2. ○ I believe men are …
3. ○ I believe women are …
4. ○ I believe wives are …
5. ○ I believe husbands are …
6. ○ I believe children are …
7. ○ I believe mothers are …
8. ○ I believe fathers are …
9. ○ What I hate most about men is …
10. ○ What I hate most about women is …
11. ○ What I hate most about parents is …
12. ○ What I hate most about children is …
13. ○ Relationships end when …
14. ○ The best relationships are …
15. ○ I believe marriage is …
16. ○ I believe divorce is …
17. ○ I believe commitment is …

Beliefs regarding judgments:

1. ○ I judge myself most when …
2. ○ I judge others most when …
3. ○ I judge my family most when …
4. ○ I judge my boss most when …
5. ○ I judge my spouse most when …
6. ○ I can forgive myself when …
7. ○ I can forgive others when …
8. ○ I cannot forgive myself for …
9. ○ I cannot forgive others if they …

Beliefs about fears:

1. ○ I am most afraid of …
2. ○ I get most anxious when …
3. ○ I feel abandoned when …
4. ○ I fear for my safety when …
5. ○ I fear for others when …
6. ○ In order to remain safe I would …

7. ○ In order to protect those I love I would …
8. ○ I feel most safe and relaxed when …
9. ○ I know others are safe to be around when …
10. ○ I know others are not safe to be around when …

Beliefs about learning:

1. ○ The most important thing about learning is …
2. ○ I don't like to learn when …
3. ○ The most painful thing about learning is …
4. ○ People who teach / teachers are …
5. ○ My most painful learning experience was …
6. ○ All learning has to be painful or uncomfortable (Y/N)
7. ○ I learn best when …
8. ○ I have never learned to …
9. ○ I cannot learn to …

Beliefs about personal change / development:

1. ○ I am willing to change when …
2. ○ I am most willing to listen to others when …
3. ○ I am willing to change myself when …
4. ○ I will never change if …
5. ○ I refuse to change when …
6. ○ If others want me to change I …
7. ○ Others should change because …
8. ○ Others change when …
9. ○ I change when …

Beliefs About money:

1. ○ People who have lots of money are …
2. ○ People who have lots of money must have …
3. ○ Rich peoples morals are …
4. ○ Wealthy people are …
5. ○ If I lost all my money I would …
6. ○ What I like most about money is …
7. ○ Money is …
8. ○ What I like least about money is …
9. ○ If I had lots of money I would / could …
10. ○ If I had lots of money I would lose what stress or worry …
11. ○ I would like myself more if I had more money (Y/N)

12. ○ I would be more accepted by others if I had more money (Y/N)

Beliefs about time:

1. ○ I always have lots of time when …
2. ○ I never have lots of time when …
3. ○ Time is …
4. ○ If I had more time I would …
5. ○ I feel I run out of time when …
6. ○ The relationship between time and power is …
7. ○ The relationship between time and love is …
8. ○ The relationship between time and sex is …
9. ○ I feel I have lost time when …
10. ○ Others control my available time when …
11. ○ I can make time if I …
12. ○ I fear I don't have enough time when …

Beliefs about power:

1. ○ I am powerful when …
2. ○ I am not powerful when …
3. ○ Others are powerful when …
4. ○ Others are not powerful when …
5. ○ Others have more power than me when …
6. ○ I have more power than others when …
7. ○ Others have more power than I do because …
8. ○ I have more power than others because …
9. ○ I can allow myself to be how powerful?
10. ○ I can allow others to be how powerful?
11. ○ I have to make sure I am in control when …
12. ○ I can let others be in control when …
13. ○ I cannot allow others to be in control when …
14. ○ If others are in control of me I feel …
15. ○ If I control others I feel …

Beliefs about control:

1. ○ I feel in control when …
2. ○ I am in control when …
3. ○ Others control me when …
4. ○ The most important things in life to control are …
5. ○ It is important that I remain in control because …

6. ○ The most important time to be in control is …
7. ○ Control is necessary because …
8. ○ Others try to control me because …
9. ○ I try to control others because …

Beliefs about love:

1. ○ I know I am in love when …
2. ○ I know I am loved when …
3. ○ I know I have lost love when …
4. ○ I fear losing love because …
5. ○ I feel abandoned when …
6. ○ I feel emotionally vulnerable when …
7. ○ I feel most secure in love when …
8. ○ I will be loved when …
9. ○ I am accepted when I …
10. ○ I am most lovable when …
11. ○ Emotions are …

Beliefs about sex:

1. ○ Sex is important because …
2. ○ In relationships sex is important because …
3. ○ Men are … in relationship to sex
4. ○ Women are … in relationship to sex
5. ○ I enjoy sex when …
6. ○ Before marriage sex is …
7. ○ After marriage sex is …
8. ○ Sex is good because …
9. ○ Sex is bad because …
10. ○ The relationship between sex and power is …

Beliefs Worksheet: #1

Section #1: List the 5 main "things" or situations you would most like to change in yourself or in your current life:
(This tells us something of "Where you are now")

1. ____________________
2. ____________________
3. ____________________
4. ____________________
5. ____________________

For each item listed in Section #1 describe the main INTERNAL reason(s), meaning mental, emotional, value or belief reasons that you have not changed the situation:
(i.e. Fears, Current Beliefs, Lack of Motivation, Beliefs About Relationships, etc.)

1. ____________________
2. ____________________
3. ____________________
4. ____________________
5. ____________________

For each item listed in Section #1 describe the main EXTERNAL reason(s) meaning reasons outside of yourself that you have not changed the situation: *(i.e. Relationship Pressures, Societal Pressures, Lack of Money, Lack of Power, Lack of Freedom, etc.)*

1. ____________________________________
2. ____________________________________
3. ____________________________________
4. ____________________________________
5. ____________________________________

Beliefs Worksheet: #2

Section #2: List the 5 main characteristics of the positive future you would like to have: *(i.e. Freedom, Spirituality, Happiness, Power, Peace, Wealth, Professional Accomplishments, and Recognition)*. This tells us "where you want to go".

1. ____
2. ____
3. ____
4. ____
5. ____

For each item listed in Section #2 please describe the main INTERNAL emotional, mental, value or belief reason(s) you have not accomplished the envisioned goal or state:

1. ____
2. ____
3. ____
4. ____
5. ____

For each item listed in Section #2 please describe the main EXTERNAL reason(s), meaning reasons outside of yourself that you have not accomplished the envisioned goal or state:

1. ____

2. ____

3. ____

4. ____

5. ____

Appendix C: Values / Priorities Assessment Worksheet

The following statements are designed to elicit unconscious or subconscious emotional responses, information and understanding. The result of the process of completing these sentences is a method of finding unhealed / sub-conscious parts of yourself so that you can work with them. You may find several answers to each statement; this is fine, since each answer is worth contemplating. Mark off each topic with a pencil as you go. It is useful to journal as you work through the list.

Once you have identified these unconscious beliefs, feelings and programs you can use various methods discussed in the book to release them and to be free of previously limiting beliefs, emotions, expectations, perspectives and attitudes.

1. ○ My primary purpose in life is ...
2. ○ My primary goal(s) in life is / are ...
3. ○ My primary focus in life is ...
4. ○ My main life values are ...
5. ○ My main life priorities are ...
6. ○ My main family values are ...
7. ○ The most important person in my life is ...
8. ○ I am most afraid of losing ...
9. ○ I fear abandonment most from ...
10. ○ I fear not having ...
11. ○ I will never give up ...
12. ○ I would give up anything for ...
13. ○ I have to have ...
14. ○ I have to ...
15. ○ I need ...
16. ○ I cannot do without ...
17. ○ I can do without ...
18. ○ I was most hurt over the loss of ...
19. ○ Emotional fulfillment is important because ...
20. ○ I choose what my heart says over what my mind says when ...
21. ○ I choose what my mind says over my heart when ...
22. ○ I choose to do what others want me to do rather than what I want to do when ...
23. ○ How important is it that I love myself? That I love others?
24. ○ How important is it that I accept myself?
25. ○ How important is what I think and feel about myself?
26. ○ How important is what others think and feel about me?

27. ○ How important is what others say about me?
28. ○ How important is freedom?
29. ○ How important is my personal integrity?
30. ○ How important is other's integrity?
31. ○ How important is it that I can trust myself?
32. ○ How important is it that I can trust others?
33. ○ How important is it that I can rely on myself?
34. ○ How important is it that I can rely on others?
35. ○ How important is justice?
36. ○ How important is my free-will / power of choice?
37. ○ How important is attention from others?
38. ○ How important is compassion for myself?
39. ○ How important is compassion for others?
40. ○ How important is my career?
41. ○ How important is my physical health?
42. ○ How important is physical vitality?
43. ○ How important is my emotional health?
44. ○ How important is my mental health?
45. ○ How important is my spiritual health?
46. ○ How important is my family?
47. ○ How important is money?
48. ○ How important is power?
49. ○ How important is inner peace?
50. ○ How important is happiness and joy?
51. ○ How important is security?
52. ○ How important is control of my life?
53. ○ How important is it for me to control others?
54. ○ How important is sex?
55. ○ How important is time?
56. ○ How important is it that I have time alone?
57. ○ How important is time with friends?
58. ○ How important is time with family?
59. ○ How important are my emotions?
60. ○ How important are other's emotions?
61. ○ How important is my lifestyle?
62. ○ How important is my social image?
63. ○ How important is my self-image?
64. ○ How important is it that I not be socially embarrassed?
65. ○ How important a role does religion play in my life?
66. ○ How important is my connection to God / Spirit?

67. ○ How important is my spiritual development?
68. ○ How do I know when my priorities and / or values are balanced?
69. ○ How do I know when my priorities and / or values are out of balance?
70. ○ How do I know when someone else's priorities and / or values are out of balance?
71. ○ How do I usually adjust the balance of my priorities and / or values?
72. ○ The behaviors I cannot stand in others are …
73. ○ The behaviors I cannot stand in myself are …
74. ○ I respect myself when I …
75. ○ I do not respect myself when I …
76. ○ I hate people who …
77. ○ I hate myself when I …
78. ○ My primary purpose in life is
79. ○ My primary goal(s) in life is / are …
80. ○ My primary focus in life is …
81. ○ My main life values are …
82. ○ My main life priorities are …
83. ○ My main family values are …
84. ○ The most important person in my life is …
85. ○ I am most afraid of losing …
86. ○ I fear abandonment most from …
87. ○ I fear not having …
88. ○ I will never give up …
89. ○ I would give up anything for …
90. ○ I have to have …
91. ○ I have to …
92. ○ I need …
93. ○ I cannot do without …
94. ○ I can do without …
95. ○ I was most hurt over the loss of …
96. ○ Emotional fulfillment is important because …
97. ○ I choose what my heart says over what my mind says when …
98. ○ I choose what my mind says over my heart when …

Appendix D: Emotional and Relationship Boundary Mapping Exercise

The following statements are designed to elicit unconscious emotional responses, information and understanding. The result of the process of completing these sentences is a method of finding unhealed or sub-conscious parts of yourself. You may find several answers to each statement; this is fine, since each answer is worth contemplating. It is useful to mark off each item with a pencil as you go. It can be helpful to journal about the answers you get as you work through the list.

Once you have identified these unconscious beliefs, feelings and programs you can use various methods discussed in the book to release them and to be free of previously limiting beliefs, emotions, perspectives and attitudes.

1. ○ Others have the right to make decisions for me when ...
2. ○ I have no power in an interaction or relationship when ...
3. ○ Others have more power or control than I do when ...
4. ○ I have the right to stand up for myself when ...
5. ○ I feel I cannot stand up for myself when / if ...
6. ○ I lose my power when ...
7. ○ I feel I cannot take care of myself when ...
8. ○ I feel I have to take care of or support others when ...
9. ○ I feel the need to control others when ...
10. ○ I feel controlled by others when ...
11. ○ I feel powerless when ...
12. ○ Others are more powerful than I am when they ...
13. ○ I am more powerful than others when I ...
14. ○ I become afraid in interactions with others when they ...
15. ○ I become afraid in interactions with others when I ...
16. ○ I feel guilty in relationships when I ...
17. ○ I feel guilty in relationships when others ...
18. ○ I feel responsible for problems in my relationships when I ...
19. ○ I feel responsible for problems in relationships when others...
20. ○ I give up what I want in relationships when ...
21. ○ I feel vulnerable in relationships when ...
22. ○ I feel afraid in relationships when ...
23. ○ I feel weak in relationships when ...
24. ○ I feel powerful in relationships when ...
25. ○ I am most effective when I ...
26. ○ I feel needed in relationships when I ...
27. ○ I feel needed in relationships when they ...
28. ○ In order to feel safe in relationships I have to ...

29. ○ In order for me to feel secure in relationships others have to.
30. ○ I feel attacked when …
31. ○ I feel I have to defend myself when …
32. ○ I feel justified in punishing others when they …
33. ○ I feel others are justified in punishing me when I …
34. ○ Balance and fairness in relationships is …
35. ○ I know my relationships are balanced and fair when …
36. ○ I manage the balance and fairness of my relationships by …
37. ○ I always know where I stand in relationships because …
38. ○ I know where I stand in a relationship by …
39. ○ The safest place to stand in a relationship is …
40. ○ The most vulnerable place to stand in a relationship is …
41. ○ The most important aspect of my relationships is …
42. ○ The thing I cannot do without in relationships is …
43. ○ I can walk away from a relationships if …
44. ○ I fear abandonment in relationships when …
45. ○ If I am abandoned I …
46. ○ If I see someone in a difficult situation I …
47. ○ I feel like I have been victimized when …
48. ○ I can tell how I really feel in relationships when …
49. ○ I cannot tell how I really feel in relationships when …
50. ○ I can express my boundaries clearly when …
51. ○ I cannot express my boundaries clearly when …
52. ○ I protect others boundaries more than my own when …
53. ○ I expect others to respect my boundaries when …
54. ○ I have a clear perception of who I am and what I want when I..
55. ○ When others tell me who they are what they want I …
56. ○ I allow my sympathy for others to overwhelm me when …
57. ○ I feel sorry for myself or feel like a victim when …
58. ○ I am willing to fight for myself when …
59. ○ I am willing to fight for others when …
60. ○ I feel I am responsible for others when …
61. ○ I feel I am responsible for myself when …
62. ○ I feel others should be responsible for me when …
63. ○ I have to be responsible for others when …
64. ○ I should be more giving in relationships because …
65. ○ Women have more power than men because …
66. ○ Men have more power than women because …
67. ○ My mother has more power than I do because / when …
68. ○ My father has more power than I do because / when …
69. ○ My spouse has more power than I do because / when …
70. ○ I have to do what others want me to because …
71. ○ I have to do what my parents want me to because …
72. ○ I have to do what my spouse wants me to because …

73. ○ I am willing to fight for what I want when …
74. ○ I am unwilling to fight for what I want because …
75. ○ I have to do what my children want me to because …
76. ○ I do not have the right to make my own decisions because …
77. ○ My decisions are only right when …
78. ○ I cannot trust myself because …
79. ○ I cannot trust others because …
80. ○ I cannot trust myself when …
81. ○ I cannot trust others when …
82. ○ I trust others most when they …
83. ○ I trust myself most when I …
84. ○ I feel safe and secure when …
85. ○ I do not feel safe or secure when …
86. ○ I feel abandoned when …
87. ○ I know I have been abandoned when …
88. ○ I feel physically at risk or unsafe when …
89. ○ I do not feel comfortable in intimate situations because/when…
90. ○ I feel most comfortable in intimate situations when …
91. ○ I feel the need to control situations when …
92. ○ I have to be the decision maker in relationships when …
93. ○ I know better than other people because …
94. ○ I understand others better than they understand me, (Y/N)
95. ○ I feel misunderstood when …
96. ○ I am hurt when others …
97. ○ I hurt others when I …
98. ○ I respect others when they …
99. ○ I feel respected by others when they …
100. ○ I respect myself when …
101. ○ I am willing to demand others' respect when …
102. ○ I am unwilling to demand others' respect because …
103. ○ I am unwilling to lead because …
104. ○ I must lead when …
105. ○ I enjoy being alone because …
106. ○ I dislike being alone because …
107. ○ The most important person in my relationships is …
108. ○ The least important person in my relationships is …
109. ○ I judge myself in my relationships most for …
110. ○ I judge others in relationships most for …
111. ○ I feel most judged when …
112. ○ I allow other's judgments to reduce my self-respect when …
113. ○ I allow other's judgments to reduce my personal power when…
114. ○ I express myself best in relationships when …
115. ○ I cannot express myself in relationships when …
116. ○ I feel I can express my feminine side when …

117. ○ I feel I can express my masculine side when ...
118. ○ My opinion is more important than others opinions when...
119. ○ Others opinions are more important/better than mine when...
120. ○ Other people are wrong because ...
121. ○ Other people are right because ...
122. ○ I am wrong when I ...
123. ○ Others are wrong when they ...
124. ○ I feel free to choose my own path when ...
125. ○ I do not feel free to choose my own path when ...
126. ○ I feel I owe others because ...
127. ○ I feel others owe me because ...
128. ○ My emotions take me over when ...
129. ○ I feel overwhelmed when ...
130. ○ I cannot control myself when ...
131. ○ My addictions/desires cause me to lose my boundaries when.
132. ○ I feel my boundaries have been breached when ...
133. ○ I feel the need to protect myself when ...
134. ○ I feel justified in striking out at others when ...
135. ○ I feel others are justified in striking out at me when ...

John Jones Bio:

John Jones received his Bachelor of Science Degree in Sociology and Anthropology with a minor in History and did Masters Studies in Business Administration. His corporate career includes fourteen years in information systems where he variously focused in the areas of business analysis, computer programming, project management and organizational change management.

John Jones is a life coach and spiritual teacher with clients in more than 28 countries. John teaches seminars on a wide variety of topics including self-empowerment, personal transformation, consciousness and self-awareness development, development of intuitive skills, and methods of healing of emotions, relationships and child-abuse. John's passion is facilitating the transformation and healing of the world by empowering all individuals to maximize their conscious awareness and their clarity of conscious sovereignty and discernment. In addition John works with executives in a variety of organizations to solve organizational, operational, technology and human resources issues.

John is also the author of:
"Enter the Era of Empowerment: Self-Sovereignty in a Complex World."
Available at: GatherInsight.Com

"Navigating Your Life"
A 3 DVD Series of Personal Transformation Instruction
&
"Transformational Meditations"
A CD of 4 Guided Self-Healing Meditations
Available at KarmicCommunications.com

Resources:

http://www.spiritvoyage.com/blog/index.php/3-mantras-to-help-insomnia/

Farrand, Thomas Ashley, "Healing Mantras, Using sound affirmations for personal power, creativity and healing", Published by Ballantine Wellspring, The Random House Publishing Group, New York. Copyright 1999

Karpman, Stephen, M.D., "Drama Triangle" entitled "Fairy Tales and Script Drama Analysis", http://www.karpmandramatriangle.com/pdf/-DramaTriangle.pdf

Krishnamurti, Jiddhu, "The Awakening of Intelligence", HarperSanFrancisco, A division of HarperCollinsPublishers. 1973, by Krishnamurti Foundation Trust Ltd., London

Jones, John B., "Enter the Era of Empowerment, Self-Sovereignty in a Complex World", 2013 Published by: CoRecreational Media Group, Distributed Through Gather Insight

Jones, John B., "Navigating Your Life", 3 DVD Visual Educational Series, Copyright Karmic Communications, LLC, 2008, ISBN 978-0-9817641-0-8

Jung, Carl, "The Portable Jung", Edited by Joseph Campbell, The Viking Portable Library, Published By the Penguin Group 1976

81659897R00122

Made in the USA
Columbia, SC
25 November 2017